the ANGLER'S LIFE

the ANGLER'S LIFE

COLLECTING AND TRADITIONS

TEXT BY
LAURENCE SHEEHAN
PHOTOGRAPHS BY
WILLIAM STITES
with Carol Sama Sheehan and
Kathryn George Precourt

CLARKSON POTTER/PUBLISHERS

NEW YORK

Published by Clarkson Potter/Publishers,
New York, New York
Member of the Crown Publishing Group
Random House, Inc., New York,
Toronto, London, Sydney, Auckland
www.randomhouse.com

Clarkson N. Potter is a trademark
and Potter and colophon are registered
trademarks of Random House, Inc.

Printed in China

Design by Jill Armus

Library of Congress Cataloging-in-
Publication Data
Sheehan, Laurence
The Angler's Life: collecting and
traditions / text by Laurence Sheehan;
photographs by William Stites, with
Carol Sama Sheehan and Kathryn
George Precourt.—1st ed.
Includes bibliographical references
and index.
1. Fishing—Equipment and
supplies—Collectors and collecting.
2. Fishing—Collectibles. 3. Fishers—
Homes and haunts. I. Sheehan, Carol
Sama. II. Precourt, Kathryn George.
III. Title.
SH453.S47 2000
688.7'91'075—dc21   00-021311

ISBN 0-517-70874-4

10 9 8 7 6 5 4 3 2 1

First Edition

Photographs on pages 142 (top) and
144–149 by Blake Little; pages 19
(bottom right) and 181 by Fran Brennan;
pages 20 and 23 by S. A. Neff Jr.

ACKNOWLEDGMENTS

We are grateful to all the anglers who opened their homes, camps, clubs, and hearts to us as we struggled to do justice to their passion for fishing and the myriad of endeavors related to that pursuit. We especially want to thank Ed and Beth Martin and their sons, Walter and Barrett; Jack and Christie Shea and their daughter, Emily; Susan Uedelhofen, Ellen McCaleb, Woods Proctor, and Dr. Tom Hall of Camp Ginger Quill on the Au Sable River in Michigan; Nick and Mari Lyons; Phillip R. Crawford; S. A. Neff Jr.; John L. Morris and Tom Jowett of Bass Pro Shops; Ron Hickman; Nancy Whitney of Islamorada Fish Company; Shaun and Beverley Matthews of Twin Farms; Gary Tanner of the American Museum of Fly Fishing; Sean Sonderman; and Craig Bero of Anglers & Writers Restaurant in New York City.

Also we thank Scott Zuckerman and his family; Brian Correll; Bert and Nancy Savage of Larch Lodge; Russell Williams of the Ashfield Rod & Gun Club; Bill Perlman and John Goncarz of Silver Panther Bait & Tackle Shop; Linda and Stu Davidson; Barney and Susan Bellinger of Sampson Bog Studio; and Jerry Oliver of Oliver and Gannon Associates, organizer of the Adirondack Antiques Show.

Thanks to Mike Farrior and all the members of the Tuna Club; Chris and Iris Clarke; Robert Wells of Cabbage Key; Captain Dave Brown; Captain Albert Ponzoa; Richard Stanczyk of Bud 'n Mary's Fishing Marina; and Captain Gary Weber.

And our gratitude to Mara and Roy Superior; George W. Cannon Jr. of River Ranch; Dick Pobst; Jim Haggar of the Pere Marquette Rod & Gun Club; Jim and Tom Johnson, Scott Jones, Sean McDonald, and John Cinka of Johnsons' Pere Marquette Lodge; Chauncey Lively; Rusty Gates of Gates Au Sable Lodge; Tom Symons; Matt Supinski of Gray Drake Lodge; Hoagy Carmichael; Jack Dennis of the Jackson Hole One-Fly; Ken Reback; and especially Jim Brown, for his guidance of us during this project, and for his and his wife Pat's hospitality on several occasions.

For the wonderful design of this book, we thank Marysarah Quinn, Lauren Monchik, Maggie Hinders, and especially Jill Armus. Thanks also to our copy editors, Mark McCauslin and Donna Ryan, and production supervisor, Joy Sikorski. For general editorial acumen and moral support, we relied as always on Lauren Shakely, this time ably and amiably assisted by Olivia Silver.

Last but not least, thanks again to our agents and faithful friends, Gayle Benderoff and Deborah Geltman.

CONTENTS

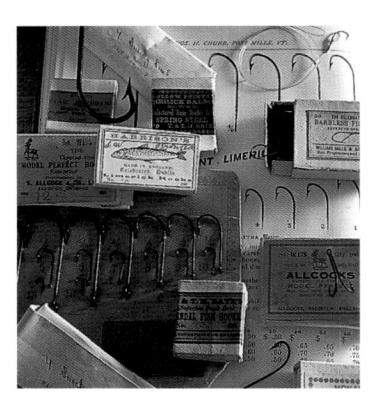

INTRODUCTION

**T**HE TWO HULKING SHADOWS gliding across the field toward our house were a chilling sight. They appeared to be armed with long pikes. It was a late-summer evening and the sun was fading below the Berkshire foothills in the western sky. We had been in the house a month. Creatures of an urban and suburban world, we were still getting used to the disquieting stillness of life in the rural countryside of western Massachusetts. Events that were ordinary in the country—a flock of wild turkeys roosting in a tree, an orchestra of cicadas taking over the night, a cow blocking the way in the road—took on an unsettling air, almost one of foreboding in our city-slicker eyes.

The figures moved out of the gloaming into a ring of soft illumination created by the lights in the house. I was considering my options for self-defense when it suddenly occurred to me that these two figures were in fact just two men in waders, carrying fly rods. And that's how we met our neighbor, Jack Shea. He and a friend had been working the Bear River, a slip of a trout stream that winds in and out of the woods from his house, about a mile away, to ours, for the past two hours.

According to the U.S. Fish and Wildlife Service, there are more than 35 million recreational anglers in America, who spend on the order of $40 billion directly on fishing trips and gear every year. Fishermen in the United States nail the "Gone Fishing" sign on their front doors a total of 626 million days, says the American Sportfishing Association. The term "sportfishing" covers a multitude of angling forms. There is deep-sea fish-

> IT WAS KIND OF
>
> ....
>
> LAZY AND JOLLY,
>
> ....
>
> LAYING OFF
>
> ....
>
> COMFORTABLE ALL
>
> ....
>
> DAY, SMOKING
>
> ....
>
> AND FISHING,
>
> ....
>
> AND NO BOOKS
>
> ....
>
> NOR STUDY.
>
> ....
>
> —*Huckleberry Finn*

ing from high-tech boats, a pursuit, however, that has become so mechanized and computerized that George Plimpton describes it as "searching for midget submarines." It is also deemed politically incorrect by environmentalists because most of the submarines—target species like swordfish, marlin, tuna, and shark—are greatly depleted in the wild, some facing extinction. There is the uniquely American world of professional bass fishing, a warm-water pursuit complete with champions whose likenesses appear on boxes of Wheaties. The original Pro Bass Tour, sponsored by the Bass Anglers Sportsman Society (BASS), was founded in the 1960s and has grown to more than half-a-million active members, with the top anglers earning substantial incomes. A relative newcomer is the Wal-Mart FLW Tour, which literally handed out suitcases full of cash to its winners in one year amounting to almost $4 million.

Opposite: JOSEPH UEDELHOFEN WAS ABOUT ELEVEN WHEN THIS SNAPSHOT, NOW TREASURED BY HIS CHILDREN, WAS TAKEN IN THE LATE 1930S. ALTHOUGH HE GREW UP IN SUBURBAN ILLINOIS, JOE'S FAMILY TOOK ANNUAL THREE-WEEK SUMMER VACATIONS ON LAKE MUD HEN IN NORTHWEST WISCONSIN, AND THERE HE LEARNED TO FISH WITH INCREASING SUCCESS.

Above: IN THE CORNER OF
ADIRONDACK FURNITURE MAKER
BARNEY BELLINGER'S STUDIO
ARE GATHERED ARTIFACTS OF
THE REGION'S UNIQUE FISHING
TRADITIONS, INCLUDING A
CHROMOLITHOGRAPH OF FIVE
BROOK TROUT FROM THE 1920S,
OLD STATE SIGNS, AND ONE
UNLUCKY SQUIRREL.

Below: SMALL FLY ROD LURES
FROM THE 1930S, SUCH AS THESE
HEDDON PUNKIE-SPOOK LURES,
RECOMMENDED FOR BASS AND
PANFISH, ARE COVETED FISHING
COLLECTIBLES.

* * *

Right: IN A CHILDREN'S RITE OF
SPRING, EMILY SHEA AND BAR-
RETT MARTIN HUNT FOR TROUT
IN THE BEAR RIVER NEAR THEIR
HOMES IN ASHFIELD, IN THE
BERKSHIRE FOOTHILLS OF WEST-
ERN MASSACHUSETTS.

Like NASCAR racing, bass fishing for dough is a hugely popular sport in Dixie. "That a man could fish for a living, could be a professional fisherman," writes Geoffrey Norman in *Sports Afield*, "made him into something special, just the way that being able to drive a car fast for a living made Richard Petty into a legend."

But as the eminent Scottish author Andrew Lang once observed in his collection *Angling Sketches*, "Next to being an expert, it is well to be a contented duffer," and the vast majority of fishermen in America are not in it for money, fame, or trophy fish; they are contented amateurs, using light tackle to pursue game fish in lakes and ponds, in rivers and streams, and, in numbers greater than ever before, in the waters near shore along the eastern seaboard, the Gulf of Mexico, and the Pacific Coast. The angling life, for them, is this and more, for it infiltrates the home, club, and camp, in the form of collections and mementos of the sport, and it colors friendships and careers.

Jack Shea—our nocturnal trespasser from down the road—teaches art and manages the outdoor program at Eaglebrook, a nearby private school for boys. A man of many parts, he operates his own sugarhouse when the sap starts flowing in his maple trees in March, hunts birds with his black Lab, Melon (who points and retrieves), every fall, and guides fishing trips to Alaska in the summer. A lifelong angler, he and his wife, Christie, have one son and three daughters, the youngest, Emily, being his latest fly-fishing protégée; she joined her father on his most recent trip to Alaska in quest of Pacific salmon and northern pike.

Because I grew up in a household that treated prizefighting with almost as much reverence as the Pope, I was astonished to learn that Jack was also a grandson of the redoubtable Jack Sharkey, a former world heavyweight champion who fought in Yankee Stadium with the likes of Joe Louis, Jack Dempsey, and Max Schmeling (defeating the last named). My father probably saw every one of his fights! I plied Jack for details.

"After retiring from the ring, Sharkey moved to Epping, New Hampshire, where he became known as the Squire of Epping," Jack relates. "I remember, going up there as a kid and rummaging around the house, being so impressed with the *stuff*—the framed photographs of him with other famous people, jars of 50-cent pieces, silver platters and other trophies, closets full of fishing gear—it was like a museum. He had a desk where he tied his own trout flies. He and Ted Williams of Boston Red Sox (and angling) fame used to put on fly-fishing exhibitions at winter trade shows for anglers in Boston and New York. They were both great fly casters. Williams, who was actually taller than Sharkey, always liked to punch the old heavyweight on the arm, to kind of needle him. And, one day, my grandfather lost his patience, and knocked out the Splendid Splinter with one punch."

What! My father's boxing hero clobbers my childhood baseball hero? Could it get any worse than that? But I put those sordid details out of mind as I found out more about Shea's relentless pursuit of the life of the outdoors, and his quiet but effective efforts to proselytize on its behalf.

Fishing was important to Jack long before he found out that

Below: THE KITCHEN IN THE CHESAPEAKE BAY COTTAGE OF SPORTING ARTIST C. D. CLARKE FEATURES A MORTEN FADUM CARVING OF STRIPED BASS, THE BAY'S PREMIER GAME FISH, ON A WINE CABINET, AS WELL AS A LOCAL CANVASBACK DUCK DECOY, FOUND IN A SHED WHEN CLARKE AND HIS WIFE MOVED TO THE AREA.

Above: BAIT BUCKETS FROM THE 1920S TO THE '50S, APPEALING IN THEIR JAUNTY PRACTICALITY, HAVE COLLECTORS TURNING ATTICS AND GARAGES UPSIDE DOWN TO FIND THEM.

* * *

Overleaf: EMILY SHEA, TUTORED BY HER ANGLING FATHER, JACK, HAS BEEN FLY-FISHING WITH GRACE AND ACCURACY SINCE SHE WAS EIGHT; HERE SHE CASTS AMONG THE BOULDERS IN THE WILCOX HOLLOW SECTION OF THE DEERFIELD RIVER IN WESTERN MASSACHUSETTS.

Below: MOST FISHERMEN ENJOY THE SOLITUDE OF THEIR SPORT MORE THAN ANY OTHER SINGLE FEATURE OR CONDITION, BUT EXCEPTIONS CAN BE MADE FOR INVITING A WELL-BEHAVED DOG ALONG FOR THE TRIP, SUCH AS JACK SHEA'S MELON, A LABRADOR RETRIEVER WHO ALSO HAS A GIFT FOR POINTING BIRDS. SHEA GREW UP IN SHELBURNE FALLS, MASSA-CHUSETTS, WITH THE DEERFIELD RIVER LITERALLY IN HIS BACK-YARD. HE BECAME A FLY FISHER-MAN MORE THAN TEN YEARS AGO.

Above: A CHEST HOLDING JACK SHEA'S FISHING GEAR WAS DECORATED FOR HIM BY HIS MOTHER, DOT, AN ARTIST, AND TESTIFIES TO HIS PASSION FOR HUNTING AS WELL AS FISHING. IN AN INCREASINGLY INFORMAL SOCIETY, AND ESPECIALLY WITH THE RAPID GROWTH OF SECOND HOMES, FURNITURE, ART, AND ACCESSORIES THAT REPRESENT AN INTEREST IN WILDLIFE AND THE GREAT OUTDOORS ARE MOVING FRONT AND CENTER WITHIN LIVING SPACES.

his grandfather also liked it. He grew up in the town of Shelburne Falls on the Deerfield River, and he has fished just about every stretch of that river from the Green Mountains of Vermont, where it originates, to the point south of Greenfield, Massachusetts, where it spills into the Connecticut River. In topography, the river valley is more reminiscent of mountainous West Virginia than of the heavily urbanized coastal regions of Massachusetts, Connecticut, and New York, and it is still almost as sparsely pop-ulated as it was when Jack was a boy.

"Our yard backed up to the river and I'd camp out there with my buddies the night before opening day of fishing season every April," he recalls. "A shed in the yard became our clubhouse."

It was not all that different, in fact, from the quintessential fishing experience of American boys as captured by Mark Twain, with his indelible characters of the frontier, Huck and Jim, baiting a big hook with a skinned rabbit and catching a 6-foot catfish, "as big a fish as was ever catched in the Missis-sippi, I reckon—Jim said he hadn't ever seen a bigger one." Or Huck, Tom Sawyer, and Joe Harper running away from home to play pirates on an island in the river 3 miles south of Hannibal, Missouri, where they hunted for turtle eggs, made tea, and caught some handsome bass for breakfast: "They fried the fish with bacon and were astonished; for no fish had ever seemed so delicious before." When they got tired of being pirates the boys decided to be Indians: "And behold they were glad they had gone into savagery . . ."

The river running through my own boyhood, Mill River in Hamden, Connecticut, was once a decent trout stream, but it has been reduced to functioning as a supplier of drinking water, and channelized to the point where it has lost most of its wetlands, not to mention most of its fish, and at some times of the year it runs almost dry. Yet it will remain forever in memory as the place where my friends and I went into "savagery," building teepees and rafts, conducting rock fights with the boys on the other side of the river in North Haven, and spearing bottom-feeding suck-ers. Like Huck, Tom, and Joe, we tried frying our fish on the campfire, not to find out until years later that the variety of suck-ers in Mill River was notoriously inedible. I think I was the one who got sick first.

Jimmy Carter might seem at first glance to have nothing in common with the first great presidential sportsman, Teddy Roosevelt, but he grew up in rural Plains, Georgia, where hunt-ing and fishing were part of daily life, and he has a profound understanding of what it is like to live on the rim of the wild. "During the Depression years, particularly among the poorer families," he writes in his memoir *An Outdoor Journal*, "hunt-ing and fishing were not looked on as sports but as necessary rest times from fieldwork and a valuable means to supplement the standard farm diet with meat." In later years, he and his wife, Rosalynn, became enthusiastic and skillful fly fishers, but as a child, he was very much in the Huck Finn mode as angler: lake fishing for perch with cane poles, using pond worms, crawfish tails, or catalpa worms for bait, and avoiding at all costs the fear-some alligator gar, a vicious-looking fish with savage teeth. "One

Left: PERHAPS THE MOST DESIR-
ABLE, AND EXPENSIVE, FORM OF
ANGLING MEMORABILIA IS FOUND
IN FISHING PAINTINGS OF THE
18TH AND 19TH CENTURIES, SUCH
AS THIS OIL ON CANVAS FROM
BERT SAVAGE'S LARCH LODGE. IT
WAS PAINTED BY MAINE ARTIST
WALTER M. BRACKETT IN 1881,
WITH A CARVED FRAME, CIRCA
1910, ATTRIBUTED TO ARTHUR
GRINNELL OF NEW BEDFORD,
MASSACHUSETTS.

Above: FLY FISHERMEN LIKE JACK
SHEA CAST WITH ARTIFICIAL
FLIES THAT RESEMBLE THE
INSECT LIFE HATCHING ON THE
RIVER AT THE TIME.

* * *

Left: IN A CONTRAST OF ANGLING
TRADITIONS, A CHERRYWOOD
PADDLE, HAND-CUT AND PAINTED
WITH BERRY PIGMENTS BY PENN-
SYLVANIA WINNEPASAUKEE
INDIANS IN 1890, IS THE BACK-
DROP FOR SEVERAL PAGES FROM
A WELL-TO-DO ENGLISHMAN'S
JOURNAL OF THE 1870S.

Below: SALTWATER FISH CAN BE CAUGHT WITHOUT LICENSE, BOAT, GUIDE, OR VERY MUCH WORK IN FLORIDA FROM BRIDGES ALL ALONG THE ATLANTIC COAST, THE GULF OF MEXICO COAST, AND IN THE FLORIDA KEYS. ALTHOUGH MOST BRIDGES ARE NOT DIRECTLY ON THE OCEAN OR THE GULF, THEY PROVIDE ACCESS TO A HOST OF SALTWATER SPECIES, INCLUDING GROUPER, SNAPPER, TARPON, AMBERJACKS, BARRACUDA, AND SHARK.

Above: BELOW THE MAIN STREET BRIDGE ON THE MILL RIVER IN DOWNTOWN STAMFORD, CONNECTICUT, JIM BROWN USES A 9-FOOT FOUR-WEIGHT ROD TO FISH CLOSE TO THE BOTTOM WITH A SMALL BEAD-HEAD NYMPH FOR HIS LURE.

✳ ✳ ✳

Right: FLY-FISHING FOR BONEFISH IN THE FLORIDA KEYS CALLS FOR AN ARTFUL COLLABORATION BETWEEN GUIDE, WHO SIGHTS THE PREY FROM HIS ELEVATED PLATFORM, AND ANGLER, WHO MUST CAST WITH SKILL AND PRECISION.

Above: THE DEN OF AN ANGLER IS STREWN WITH TACKLE USED ON A DAILY BASIS AS WELL AS ODDS AND ENDS COLLECTED AS SOUVENIRS OF THE SPORT AND ITS TRADITIONS, INCLUDING A COPY OF *CONFESSIONS OF A CARP FISHER*, A FAVORITE AMONG POLITICALLY INCORRECT ANGLERS FROM ENGLAND.

Carter's fishing hero growing up was one Rachel Clark, an undersized black girl who took snuff and laughed a lot, "and was also known as the finest fisher in the neighborhood." The young Carter would dig worms and collect caterpillars to get Rachel to let him tag along with her on fishing trips into the woods. "Then we were off to Choctawhatchee or Kinchafoonee Creek or to Hog Branch," he reports, evoking the seductive mixed-bag culture of his Deep South, "sometimes walking five miles or more before we arrived at the creek bank." It was a foregone conclusion that Rachel would catch more fish, but Carter says he was "never tempted to be jealous or envious, so great was her skill. I carried my fish on a stripped willow limb threaded through the gills; Rachel put hers in a kind of creel made out of a white flour sack."

Although some of the anglers in this book are autodidacts, most of them came by fishing through the generosity and the gift of mentoring of a person like Rachel Clark, usually some childhood friend or relative.

"In my family, a thirteenth birthday decided not whether a child was an adult, but whether he or she would become a fisherman," writes Janna Bialek in *Uncommon Waters*, a book of essays by women anglers. "At that age we were allowed to accompany our grandparents on their annual trek to southern Ontario, joining that mysterious fraternity of fishing people that only an adolescent could covet with such romantic imagination."

Bialek recalls her first summer fishing on Lake Huron with her grandfather and a guide named Cecil, "a handsome Indian with white hair and only one leg. . . . Cecil would sit in our boat, watching the water, never giving advice but always knowing exactly the right thing to do if asked. He was part of the machinery that kept us fishing, but more than that, he made what we were doing seem somehow very old and important."

Several years ago, Jack Shea achieved the same effect by designing an elective course in fly-tying for sixth-graders at his school. "The class is limited to six kids and we meet five days a week for thirty-five minutes," he explains. "We build our own fly bench, dress from twelve to twenty flies, and try them out on the school pond, stocked with about 150 rainbows and browns." As their confidence and self-esteem grows, Shea has seen kids awaken, not just to angling, but to natural history and the outdoor world in all its aspects. "If I hook one, he is my friend through ninth grade."

The angler's life is about failure more often than success, however. More than a century ago, Andrew Lang expressed this fact of fishing life with characteristic bemusement as he considered his own unbounded zeal for the thing:

"Perhaps it is an inherited instinct, without the inherited power," he reflected. "I may have had a fishing ancestor who bequeathed to me the passion without the art. My vocation is fixed, and I have fished to little purpose all my days."

1

FISHING
ROOMS

THIS EVOCATIVE LINE from the Prague-born poet and novelist Rilke is scrawled across one of a set of nine large paintings that engulf the visitor in abstract images of the wilderness on his visit to the Cy Twombly gallery, at the Menil Collection in Houston, Texas. Without depicting a single fish or a wild thing of any kind, the renowned American artist Cy Twombly uses swirls of color—the deep green of the woods, the limpid blue-green of water, "a sense of densely cool, shore-side shadow," as one critic noted—to suggest the deep woods and the uncompromising beauty of nature, shot through with light and motion. There is nothing in the room but the nine pictures, painted in oils on wood panels, and though they are titled *Untitled,* no angler can stand in their midst without

> **AND IN THE**
>
> **PONDS BROKEN**
>
> **OFF FROM THE**
>
> **SKY, MY FEELING**
>
> **SINKS AS IF**
>
> **STANDING ON**
>
> **FISHES.**
>
> —*Rainer Maria Rilke*

being prodded by Rilke's lyrical poetry into remembering some moment of peace and certainty from the past, experienced on some sapphire Adirondack lake, on a "big two-hearted river" in Michigan, on one of Florida's dazzling bonefish flats, or on that warmish farm pond fished and fished one long hot summer as a child. For a fleeting moment the gallery in the museum becomes a fishing room, a place where memory intersects with materials to produce emotion.

The German word for it is *stimmung,* "the sense of intimacy that is created by a room and its furnishings," observes architect Witold Rybczynski, in his book *Home,* "a characteristic of interiors that has less to do with functionality than with the way that the room conveys the charac-

Opposite: THE FIRST GENUINE FISHING ROOM IN THE WESTERN WORLD MAY HAVE BEEN THIS TEMPLE-LIKE EDIFICE BUILT IN 1674 ON THE DOVE RIVER IN ENGLAND, AND STILL STANDING TODAY. IT WAS ERECTED BY CHARLES COTTON, A COUNTRY SQUIRE, POET, AND ANGLER, IN TRIBUTE TO HIS ESTEEMED OLDER FRIEND IN FISHING, SIR IZAAK WALTON, AUTHOR OF *THE COMPLEAT ANGLER.*

ter of its owners—the way that it mirrors [their] soul."

So we were, in effect, soul-searching when we went looking for rooms that revealed an angling way of life, an obsessive interest in things piscatorial, an unmistakable, unquenchable passion for fishing. We were convinced that, if we could locate these places, sacred or profane, predictable or surprising, public or private, elegant or down-and-out, we would be able to hold up a universal mirror to the fisherman's soul.

If not the world's very first fishing room, a tiny building on a bend of the Dove River, which runs between Derbyshire and Staffordshire in England, is surely the most enduring. It was erected in 1674 by Charles Cotton in honor of the visit of his friend, Sir Izaak Walton, in that year, to Beresford Hall, of which Cotton was squire. A Fleet Street, London, haberdasher, Walton is best known for writing the world's most often reprinted, and least read, masterwork, *The Compleat Angler*. Cotton's streamside folly, "built foursquare of stone, with round arched doorway flanked by pilasters, square-headed windows, and pyramidal stone-tiled roof surmounted by a sundial and ball," survives more than

three centuries later, robed in time and half forgotten, a noble tribute to friendship and comity among anglers, and to angling itself.

The first fishing room in the United States was created in 1747 by the Schuylkill Fishing Company on the Schuylkill River, which, at the time, crept *en plein air* through the dirt and cobble streets of the fledgling colonial metropolis of Philadelphia and abounded in fish. It would not be for more than a century, until the period following the Civil War, that fishing clubs spread like a new disease on the rivers and lakes of the New World, but "The Castle" on the Schuylkill was the mother of them all. It was actually a simple wood building coated with peeling yellow wash and board shutters painted in imitation of Gothic windows. Only Philadelphians at the top of the city's pecking order were worthy of admission, of course, and both George Washington and General Lafayette are said to have dined here, presumably on the club china, each piece stamped with the emblem of a sun perch. The wonder is that women anglers apparently were full partners in the fishing fandango; then again, it was still a brave new world in 1747.

Above: BOOKBINDER S. A. NEFF JR.'S TRIBUTE TO CHARLES COTTON'S "FISHING HOUSE" SHOWS THE BUILDING
AGAINST THE BACKDROP OF THE DOVE RIVER, WITH THE GREEN DRAKE, *EPHEMERA DANICA*, ENGLAND'S LARGEST
MAYFLY, IN THE FOREGROUND. *Opposite:* THE DOVE, A LIMESTONE TROUT STREAM, WINDS THROUGH A
WELL-PRESERVED GREENBELT AREA IN THE INDUSTRIAL MIDLANDS NEAR LONDON.

"There is a society of sixteen ladies and as many gentlemen, called the 'Fishing Company,'" wrote an English visitor in 1759, clearly impressed with this untitled yet aristocratic little band of anglers. "They have a very pleasant room erected in a romantic situation upon the banks of that river, where they generally dine and drink tea. There are several pretty walks about it, and some wild and rugged rocks which, together with the water and fine groves that adorn the banks, form a most beautiful and picturesque scene. There are boats and fishing-tackle of all sorts, and the company divert themselves with walking, dancing, singing, conversing, going upon the water and fishing, or just as they please."

As it happens, there is a unique animating spirit behind every genuine fishing room. The passionate angler believes such a room upholds the values of the fishing experience, shapes the fishing narrative in memory, gives the sport meaning beyond the conventions of hook, line, and sinker.

"You want to be on the water all the time," explains Chris Clarke, an artist whose house on the remote salt marshes of Chesapeake Bay is filled with fishing pictures painted by Chris and by friends, "but since you can't, you might as well have it all around you."

New York restaurant owner Craig Bero, growing up in northern Wisconsin, learned all manner of woodcraft from the Native Americans who befriended him. Decades later, he built a child-sized fishing camp for himself beside a trout stream in upstate New York. With birch-bark-clad walls, a flytier's table, and old metal bait tins for crickets and grasshoppers, the camp replicates the angling customs and environment of his youth. Even the jigging stick he uses for ice-fishing was carved by an Indian back in the 1920s.

Pennsylvanian Sid Neff's bookbinding studio, a flight of stairs up from his angling library, is also the repository for his "stable" of fishing rods, as he calls it, a collection of Austrian fishing hats bedecked with angling badges and medallions, and a well-stocked flytier's desk. Neff's studio is as much a reflection of the angler as his magnificent library.

Jim Brown, a librarian by trade, hasn't much room at

Opposite: THE SUMMER RETREAT OF CALIFORNIA ARTIST JACK BAKER ON MAINE'S ST. GEORGE PENINSULA BECKONS VISITORS WITH ITS RUSTIC ARCHED DOOR AND SEEN-HARD-TIMES FISH TROPHY. *Above:* ANGLING WHAT-NOTS, INCLUDING AN OLD ICE-FISHING SPEAR, CASUALLY SHARE SPACE WITH GARDEN TOOLS IN A BREEZEWAY AT BEAR RIVER FARM, MASSACHUSETTS. *Overleaf:* ONE OF SPORTING ARTIST SCOTT ZUCKERMAN'S FAVORITE FISHING ROOMS IS HIS OWN PORCH. THE OLD RATTAN ROCKING CHAIR WAS RESTORED AND PAINTED BY JOANNE ZUCKERMAN.

all left in the small chamber in his home that is packed with the desiderata of his fishing passions. His totemic fly reel collection now competes for space with a new interest, fly-fishing lures by the thousands, antic little engines of deceit dating from the 1920s, '30s, and '40s. One of his proudest possessions, the likeness of a trophy 8½-pound brown trout that Jim caught in 1996 in Labrador, exquisitely carved by a friend, Steve Smith, is still wrapped in makeshift padding while waiting for wall space to open up.

Such "proof of prowess," as President Herbert Hoover, a devoted fisherman in his day, called taxidermy, often suffered rejection at home in the old days. In *Fishing for Fun*, Hoover provided a cautionary chapter on the business of preserving prize specimens hooked in exotic fishing locations: "After he is stuffed and you have paid the bill and the freight and truck charges, you must mount him over the living-room mantel, where you hope he will provide a conversational item, and that all your guests will marvel." But Hoover concludes, "By and by your wife disapproves of him as a household ornament and insists he has moths. Anyway, she bribes the garbage man with five dollars to take him away while you are at the office."

Apart from the fact that today's "little woman" is as likely to be catching trophy fish as a man, most contemporary angling families would be proud to exhibit a beautifully carved fish, such as Jim's brownie, on a wall in the house. More than ornament, such workmanship invites being called art.

Writing of his efforts to create durable emblems of the angling experience in a cabin he shared with a friend in the Catskills in the 1930s, John McDonald, author of the seminal fly-fishing work, *Quill Gordon*, explained, "We casually put our larger trout on the cabin wall, tracing the shape of the trout on a piece of paper and then transferring it in ink line drawing on the faded old wallpaper, writing in the name of who had caught it, the date, and attaching the fly or record to the nose of the outlined trout."

McDonald could not bear to leave behind such a powerful souvenir of his and his friend's exploits when the cabin was abandoned in 1941, so he hacked the whole thing out of the wall and took it home to be framed.

In the case of Charles Cotton, this was a man described by one biographer as "a careless, open handed, seventeenth century squire, fond of his jest, his flagon of ale, and his pipe of tobacco . . . above all, a prince of fly-fishers to whom the whole angling fraternity is forever indebted."

Indeed, by modern standards, Cotton was much more of a stand-up fly-fishing kind of guy than his older friend Walton, who used worms to catch fish. Cotton was a firm believer in presenting to trout, which come to the surface to feed more than any other fish, imitations of the insects that constitute their natural fare. He wrote a treatise on the subject, "How to Angle for Trout or Grayling in a Clear Stream," in 1676, complete with a list of sixty-five flies and how to tie them. Sir Izaak was so impressed that he asked Cotton to write the second part of the fifth edition of his own tome in the same year. Cotton had only ten days to produce the work, but he met the deadline. Thus the clandestine art of fly-fishing became a part and parcel of the angling classic. He even included a recipe for poaching trout using stale beer vinegar, white wine, horseradish, and "a handsome little faggot of rosemary, thyme and winter savory."

Of all forms of light-tackle fishing, fly-fishing seems to attract the most collectors and connoisseurs. "No sport lives daily in its heritage more intimately than fly-fishing," says Nick Lyons. It may just boil down to the fact that an artificial fly tied out of exotically colored materials looks better in a marbled frame than does an earthworm.

But if we are speaking of fishing rooms, it is better to conclude with the lines of Charles Cotton himself, composed while on a wearying eighteenth-century business trip in London and sick for home:

My river still through the same channel glides
Clear from the tumult, salt and dirt of tides
And my poor Fishing-house, my seat's best grace
Stands firm and faithful in the self-same place.

CAMP GINGER QUILL

RIVER REFUGE ON THE STORIED AU SABLE

THE LIVING ROOM seemed to glow even when there was no fire," recalls Frederick B. Smith Jr., grandson of Henry B. Smith, a Bay City, Michigan, attorney and sportsman who built Camp Ginger Quill on the Au Sable River in northern Michigan in 1928. That quintessential fishing room is still the soul of the camp, with its tobacco-stained stucco walls, outsized doors and windows, and immense native stone fireplace. The retreat, blending rusticity with elegance, was created in a tradition that began with the proliferation of plush wilderness camps in the Adirondacks in the 1880s and soon spread westward. Even its name was an import: the trout fly called ginger quill, indigenous to the eastern United States, does not live on Michigan's rivers.

Originally consisting of seven structures located on 160 acres, Ginger Quill was divided after the Smith family gave it up and portions sold off to separate owners in the late 1960s. Ignominiously, it served as a bachelor pad during one interval, gussied up with feminine comforts to seduce young women instead of trout, but a collective of seven hard-core Michigan anglers took it over and corrected course. One of them, Tom Opre, a reporter, evoked the traditional character to which Ginger Quill had been restored in a tribute he wrote in the twenty-fifth anniversary issue of *Michigan Trout* in 1984. Describing the

Opposite: MICHIGAN'S MOST FAMOUS TROUT RIVER, THE AU SABLE, IS A CLASSIC DRY-FLY STREAM, EASILY ACCESSIBLE TO THE ANGLER, WITH A PROLIFIC INSECT LIFE VIRTUALLY UNMATCHED IN THE MIDWEST.

* * *

Below: A 1971 DRAWING OF THE AU SABLE RIVERBOAT HANGS IN ONE OF THE CLUB ROOMS.

Left: GINGER QUILL, ON THE SOUTH BANK OF THE MIDDLE BRANCH, OR AU SABLE MAIN-STREAM, IS BLESSED WITH CREA-TURE COMFORTS, SUCH AS A BAR AND A GAME ROOM (AND PLUMB-ING), UTTERLY LACKING IN THE FIRST FISHING CAMPS AND LODGES BUILT ALONG THE AU SABLE, FOLLOWING THE ARRIVAL OF THE RAILROAD IN GRAYLING, MICHIGAN, IN 1879.

end of a typical day of fishing at Ginger Quill, Opre waxed, "You slog through the river back to Camp. The fly rod is placed gently on an outside rack and the waders hung up to dry. A friend may greet you at the Camp door with a drink. The smoky gold whiskey swirls in the ice cubes, and

it traces a warm trail down your throat. The heady color of sizzling steaks wafts from a charcoal grill, rising through the pines in the front yard. The river's voice is like the murmur of an old friend nearly lost somewhere in the background."

But it is the younger Smith, recalling family trips to his grandfather's home away from home, who captured the child's-eye view of the place, in an informal memoir he wrote for the present owners:

"For us the long ride from Bay City was almost over when we heard the gravel strike the underside of the car near Roscommon. Our father would make a short stop at Jack's Rod and Fly Shop to pick up flies and leaders. We would always stop on the bridge over the South Branch to say hello to the Au Sable. From there we would search for the small Camp Ginger Quill signs nailed to trees or posts, among what seemed like a hundred other signs, indicating when we should turn."

Young Fred Smith remembered waking up to breakfasts of Au Sable pancakes—balls of pancake batter deep-fried and covered with honey butter. There were daily encounters with the wildlife on the river: kingfishers, muskrats, mallards, beavers, great blue herons, broad-winged hawks, rose-breasted grosbeaks, pileated woodpeckers, whippoorwills. Evenings, the family played canasta and cribbage and followed their favorite baseball team, the Detroit Tigers, on TV.

Camp Ginger Quill's power to lull, pacify, and civilize continues unabated. Tom Opre concludes his tribute: "In the Camp's main room firelight illuminates the stained wood beams and stucco walls. The faces are happy. The talk full of laughter. What more can we ask? Friends, fish, rivers, and the wilderness around us."

URBANE ANGLER

ART- AND BOOK-LINED CITY APARTMENT

W HEN NICK LYONS was growing up in Brooklyn, New York, there was an abandoned coal bin in the basement of the building where he and his family lived. In his early teens, he swept and mopped the place and converted it into his first authentic fishing room. He papered its walls with pages torn from *Field & Stream*, *Outdoor Life*, *Sports Afield*, and *Fur, Fish and Game*—"my windows to the great world of angling beyond my gray universe," as he has described what those magazines meant to him at the time.

"I tinkered with my tackle in that tiny room for several years," he recalls. "I read my first fishing books there. I began with Ray Bergman's *Trout*, as did most fishermen I know. I was looking for some logic to it all—the never-ending stream of tackle and conflicting techniques, some understanding of the world of rivers, which I had begun to fish."

Fast-forward a half century, through a distinguished career as an English professor, book editor, and publisher, to a block of classic brownstones on the Upper West Side in Manhattan. Here, a stone's throw from Zabar's, the ultimate gourmet delicatessen, on one side, and the Hudson River, where stripers are making a welcome comeback, on the other, Nick Lyons, now the patriarch of American fly-fishing literature and lore, is still turning out elegant and witty essays on angling on his manual Royal typewriter.

But it is a western spring creek that astounds the eye when a visitor climbs a narrow staircase and turns into Nick's art- and book-filled living room. One oil painting, roughly 60 square feet of untamed Montana terrain, looms high over the fireplace. It is the work of Mari Lyons, Nick's wife of forty-two years and counting, who paints, these days in ever larger formats, in a studio that happens to be over a bagel factory in the same neighborhood. Her work has been praised in *The New Republic* and *Forbes FYI*. Known for her bold, painterly, and spacious style, Mari only in recent years has turned her eye to her husband's

Opposite: THE HOME OFFICE OF PUBLISHER, EDITOR, AND ANGLING ESSAYIST NICK LYONS SERVES BOTH AS THE REPOSITORY FOR HIS FAVORITE FISHING TITLES AND A SHOWCASE FOR THE ANGLING ART OF HIS WIFE, MARI LYONS. FOUNDER OF THE LYONS PRESS, NICK HAS TURNED OVER DAY-TO-DAY OPERATIONS OF THAT ENTERPRISE TO HIS SON, TONY, BUT CONTINUES TO RECEIVE, AND DUTIFULLY READ, AS MANY AS 700 BOOK SUBMISSIONS A YEAR, MOST OF THEM ABOUT FISHING. ABOVE THE BOOKSHELF IS MARI'S WATERCOLOR OF A BROWN TROUT, USED FOR THE JACKET OF NICK'S *CONFESSIONS OF A FLY FISHING ADDICT*.

* * *

Below: NICK'S BOOK OF ESSAYS ON WESTERN FLY-FISHING, *SPRING CREEK*, WAS ILLUSTRATED WITH WATERCOLORS BY MARI, EXECUTED ON THE RIVER. THIS EXEMPLIFIES THE KIND OF "COMMINGLING" OF THEIR SEPARATE ARTISTIC EXPRESSIONS THAT HE HAD LONG DESIRED.

Angling Books

Nick Lyons knows collecting, having amassed not one but three significant libraries of fly-fishing books in his lifetime. The first was lost in a devastating fire that reduced his New York apartment to charcoal. The second was surrendered at auction to raise tuition money when all four of his children were in college at the same time. The third collection now lends its special ambience to the room where he writes. "Collecting is the most personal of activities," he notes, "as sure a totem of one's individuality as a fingerprint."

Here are some of Nick's hard-earned observations about book collecting, as gleaned from his lively memoir, *My Secret Fishing Life* (1999, Atlantic Monthly Press).

❋ ON GETTING STARTED I began purely as an accumulator, bringing home books I'd edited for Crown, adding old books I bought to consider for republication, finding others in yard sales and library sales that merely looked interesting, and buying those, used and new, that had information I sorely wanted. The world of fly-fishing was mysterious and compelling, on and off the river, and I simply could not fish often enough, read enough about it.

❋ ON ESTABLISHING VALUE The condition of the book affects the price absolutely; the edition is impor-

ANCIENT VOLUMES SUCH AS THIS FIFTH EDITION OF *THE EXPERIENCED ANGLER OR ANGLING IMPROVED* BY COL. ROBERT VENABLE, PUBLISHED IN 1683 (AND NOW PART OF THE LIBRARY OF S. A. NEFF JR.), ARE SO RARE AND EXPENSIVE AS TO BE OUT OF THE PRICE RANGE OF MOST FISHING BOOK COLLECTORS. ACCORDING TO NEFF, THE BOOK'S FRONTISPIECE CONTAINS ONE OF THE EARLIEST KNOWN ILLUSTRATIONS OF A TROUT FLY.

tant; the importance of the book counts; and of course anything like personal letters from the author or a signature or a long inscription (and to whom—association value) will help push up the price. Always the number printed is a factor; the Derrydale Press editions were all limited press runs, and since they were generally carefully selected books and handsomely produced volumes, they're prized collector's items in the sporting field.

❋ ON BOOK DEALERS Reliable specialty dealers rather than random looking became my best single source for specific needs. The dealers knew the field well; they could advise on variant editions; they could be trusted for quality. . . . A good dealer will describe books carefully, will ship them well packaged, and will advise honorably on a variety of practical matters associated with used and rare sporting books. A dealer who once ships you an ugly, ungainly edition with foxing [brown age spots], loose pages, and even disfiguration —none of which were noted in the catalog copy—should probably never be trusted again.

❋ ON THE REMAINDER TABLE The sporting field responds quickly to the pressure of high demand and low availability; I know of a half-dozen cases within the past five years when remaindered books became worth double their list price a year after being abandoned by their not-so-knowledgeable publishers.

❋ ON THE WHY OF IT Collecting fly-fishing books enables me to explore rivers I will never fish, explore theories and practices that give great pleasure in themselves and cannot help but affect next season's sport, and live for a while in another fly-fisher's boots, brain, and heart.

consuming passion for angling and the multilayered literature of angling.

The Lyonses have traveled to rivers and streams all of their married life, and the Madison River valley has been one of their favorite destinations, although for Mari it has been an acquired taste. It was no accident that Nick, who has published more than four hundred articles and eighteen books, named one of his earlier collections of essays *Fishing Widows.*

"When I first hauled Mari to Montana," he admits, "she went reluctantly. She hated to leave her studio for a month and thought her oils and canvases too cumbersome to take along," adding, "Also, after far too many years of it, she still found the endless fish talk boring in the extreme."

Before long, however, Mari was staying on the river as long as if not longer than her husband, finding inspiration in the setting, painting landscapes over and over again in watercolors, and sketching fishing vignettes in pen and ink.

Quite unintentionally, many of these works would one day turn out to be the perfect images to illustrate Nick's writings—to the author's deep satisfaction.

"I realized that I wanted nothing more than to have our work commingled," says Nick, who has long been known for encouraging the creative work of friends and strangers alike. "And I realized too that she had finally found her connection to this odd and enduring passion of mine for rivers and for fly-fishing, through her work."

Top: A TRADITIONALIST TO THE BONE, LYONS STILL WRITES ON A MANUAL TYPEWRITER.

* * *

Above and left: A PEN-AND-INK SKETCH OF NICK LYONS AND A. J. MCCLANE, OF MCCLANE'S *ANGLING ENCYCLOPEDIA* FAME, WAS DONE IN "HALF A MINUTE," ACCORDING TO LYONS, BY HIS WIFE, WHILE THE OLD FRIENDS PROWLED FOR SPORT ON A SPRING CREEK IN MONTANA.

* * *

Overleaf: NICK LYONS'S COLLECTION OF ANGLING BOOKS RANGES FROM CLASSICS LIKE RAY BERGMAN'S *FRESH-WATER BASS* TO MORE CONTEMPORARY RIFFS ON FISH LIKE JAMES PROSEK'S *ILLUSTRATED TROUT.*

JAMES PROSEK

TROUT

Frank Elder

The Book of the Hackle

DERRYDALE PRESS

WEAVINGS ROUND THE CREEL

WILLIAM G. TAPPLY

A FLY-FISHING LIFE

NICK LYONS ✦ MARI LYONS

Fishing Bamboo

Gierach

818

FRESH-WATER
BASS

BERGMAN

PENN

ELLIS

THE
ATLANTIC
SALMON

LEE WULFF

DEN OF ANTIQUITY

SPORTING HERITAGE OF ABERCROMBIE & FITCH

T HE FAMILY ROOM of New Hampshire collector Phillip Crawford is a time capsule of blue-blood American sporting style of the early twentieth century. It is literally filled to the roof beams with the products and paraphernalia of the original Abercrombie & Fitch flagship store in Manhattan, one of America's most famous and colorful retailers.

"The slide only began in the late 1960s, when what had been the greatest sporting goods store in the world went from leather to leatherette," relates Crawford, who first became interested in the emporium when he picked up an old wicker picnic set with the A&F logo on it at a secondhand store in 1980.

"That logo stood for quality and service in the old days, a name brand as respected as Tiffany," Crawford says. "After all, the store had been the outfitter for Teddy Roosevelt, Admiral Richard Byrd, Ernest Hemingway. . . . In World War I even the Red Cross got their uniforms from Abercrombie & Fitch. But the old market of well-heeled hunters, fishers, and campers fell off over the years. On November 14, 1977, the flagship store in Manhattan was closed. Anything in the store that wasn't sold off went to auction—catalogs, fixtures, furniture, soft goods that had been returned, you name it."

It was a sorry end to an enterprise that blazed many new trails in the manufacture and merchandising of sporting goods over the years. In fact, when Abercrombie & Fitch opened its store in a twelve-story building at the corner of Madison Avenue and Forty-fifth Street in 1917, it's

sign read: "Where the Blazed Trail Crosses the Boulevard." On the roof of the new store was a log cabin and a casting pool. Other floors had dog kennels, a rifle range, and tent exhibits, including one with an actual campfire blazing in the corner.

Acquiring, mostly at auctions, twenty to forty items a year, from A&F ashtrays and lighters to Payne rods and Hardy reels, Crawford gradually built up his present collection of nearly 2,000 pieces. It includes the

Opposite: THE MAHOGANY FLY-TIER'S DESK WITH BRASS FITTINGS WAS CUSTOM BUILT FOR PHILLIP CRAWFORD TO SHOW OFF THE FLY-TYING GEAR AND MATERIALS MADE AND SOLD BY THE ORIGINAL ABERCROMBIE & FITCH. THE OPEN BOOK BEHIND THE VISE IS MARY ORVIS MARBURY'S CLASSIC *FAVORITE FLIES AND THEIR HISTORIES,* 1892. IN ADDITION TO ALL ITS STANDARD OFFERINGS FOR THE OUTDOORSMAN, A&F ALSO STOCKED SUCH EXOTIC SPORTING EQUIPMENT AS HOT AIR BALLOONS, THROWING KNIVES, AND PORTABLE TRAMPOLINES.

Left: A PIONEER IN THE MAIL-ORDER CATALOG BUSINESS, ABERCROMBIE & FITCH SOLD ITS GOODS WORLDWIDE. BUT ITS MOST SATISFIED CUSTOMERS CAME TO THE STORE IN PERSON. "OLD-TIMERS AS WELL AS YOUNG FELLOWS FIND IT A REAL TREAT TO VISIT OUR SHOP AND TALK FISH, CAMP, AND VACATION," DECLARED AN EARLY CATALOG FROM ITS CHICAGO STORE. "WE ARE ALWAYS READY TO HELP AND ADVISE, WHETHER YOU PLAN AN EXTENDED CANOE TRIP TO THE WILDS OF CANADA, OR A WEEK-END TRIP TO THE NEAREST TROUT STREAM."

thirteen framed covers of early catalogs that originally hung in the A&F board-room, a library of the forty-two classic sporting books that were reprinted under the A&F name, and such oddities as a marbleized tool for oiling fishing reels, a collection of fish knives, and a compact travel fly rod made in 1915.

The business had been started in 1892 by David T. Abercrombie, an out-doorsman from Baltimore, with a knack for designing tents, rucksacks, and other camping equipment. In 1900, one of his many loyal customers, Ezra Fitch, talked Abercrombie into making him his partner. Fitch was a lawyer from Kingston, New York, who loved trekking in the Adirondacks and wanted more Americans, most of whom were devoted homebodies, to enjoy the benefits of outdoor activities. By all accounts, both men were stubborn, hot-tempered individuals, and by 1907 the founder had had enough of the arguing: Abercrombie resigned.

Under Fitch the store expanded into sportswear, for women as well as men, and launched a pioneering mail-order business, eventually reaching 50,000 customers around the world, including the Duke of Windsor, Howard Hughes, and Greta Garbo. A&F was where Cole Porter ordered his evening clothes. During Prohibition, it was the place to buy hip flasks.

Fitch resigned from the business in 1928, to return to trips in the great out-doors that he loved so much, and A&F continued to prosper in service to its customers for decades. "Old-timers, as well as young fellows, find it a real treat to visit our shop and talk fish, camp and vacation," declared an early catalog from the Chicago store. "We are always ready to help and advise, whether you plan an extended canoe trip to the wilds of Canada, or a weekend trip to the nearest trout stream."

Reincarnated in 1988 as a chain of casual clothing stores for twenty-somethings, Abercrombie & Fitch enjoyed success anew in the 1990s, although the original partners, wandering into one of the chain's many new boutiques, might well have asked, "Where's the campfire?"

Left: AT ONE TIME THE LARGEST
SPORTING GOODS STORE IN THE
WORLD, ABERCROMBIE & FITCH
CARRIED RODS, REELS, HOOKS,
LINE, LURES, AND EVERYTHING
ELSE REQUIRED FOR SALT- OR
FRESHWATER FISHING, ALONG
WITH PRODUCTS OF ITS OWN
DESIGN, SUCH AS POCKET HAND
WARMERS. FLAGS FOR FISHING
BOATS WERE USED TO SIGNAL THE
DAY'S RESULTS UPON RETURNING
TO DOCK; SHOWING THE SKUNK
MEANT YOU WERE COMING BACK
WITHOUT A FISH.

* * *

Below: A&F DICTATED TASTE FOR
GENERATIONS OF AMERICAN
ANGLERS, NOT ONLY IN WHAT
KIND OF EQUIPMENT FISHERMEN
USED ON THE STREAM, FROM
REELS TO CREELS TO LANDING
NETS, BUT HOW THEY FUR-
NISHED THEIR GAME ROOMS,
DENS, AND OFFICES.

Left: FLY REELS WERE MADE FOR ABERCROMBIE & FITCH BY HARDY BROTHERS, ALNWICK, NORTHUMBERLAND, ENGLAND, SINCE THE 1870S CONSIDERED BY MANY TO BE THE PREEMINENT MAKER OF TROUT AND SALMON REELS IN GREAT BRITAIN, IF NOT THE WORLD. A&F WAS ALSO AN IMPORTANT RETAIL OUTLET FOR AMERICAN CUSTOM REEL MAKERS INCLUDING CHARLES M. CLINTON OF ITHACA, NEW YORK, HARRY MCVICKAR OF TUXEDO PARK, NEW YORK, AND STANLEY BOGDAN OF NASHUA, NEW HAMPSHIRE; THEIR HANDIWORK FOR A&F CARRIED THE STORE NAME AND LOGO.

* * *

Below: POCKET KNIVES, FISHING KNIVES, AND OTHER UTILITY KNIVES, CUSTOM MADE BY NOTEWORTHY AMERICAN KNIFE MAKERS, WERE AN A&F SPECIALITY.

* * *

Bottom: A FISHING BOAT PENNANT TO MARK A SUCCESSFUL OUTING IN SALTWATER.

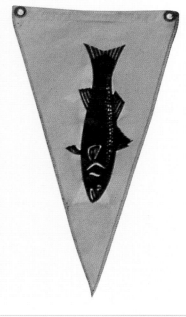

MAGNIFICENT OBSESSION

ANGLING LIBRARY OF A MASTER BOOKBINDER

WITH TRIBAL Oriental rugs underfoot and collections of nineteenth-century fish art, salmon and trout flies, and salmon and sea trout reels on walls and shelves, the library of S. A. Neff Jr., bookbinder extraordinaire, is a richly textured chamber of angling past and present. Located on an upper floor of Neff's Victorian house in western Pennsylvania, the room also contains piscatorial postcards, as he calls them, in the hundreds, a unique set of early-nineteenth-century woodblocks depicting fishes, and a decade's worth of his own angling and travel journals and personal diaries.

Neff has traveled and fished in many places, including Ireland (where he lived and worked for several years), Scotland, England, Central Europe, and the American West. He is an accomplished photographer; his lectures on fishing, illustrated with his own 35mm slides, are genial, thoroughly informed meditations on the history and mysterious appeal of the sport. "Fishing, above all, is a spiritual experience," he declares.

For all his achievements, Sid Neff is best known for his bookbinding, an ancient craft he took up when he was in his forties. He made up for the late start with the same fanatical zeal he brings to cataloging his library of more than 2,000 fishing titles, the earliest dating from 1600.

Collectors of angling books are as attentive to the quality and condition of the bindings of their old fishing books as they are to the words within, whether those bindings are of the finest vellum made from calf, or cloth. But when they come upon Neff's bookbinding for the first time, they are usually at a complete loss for words. The craftsmanship is as impressive as the complex conceptual thinking underpinning it.

Above: FOR THE BOOK *A TREASURY OF REELS* BY JIM BROWN, NEFF CREATED A KIND OF TREASURE CHEST WITH A BAS-RELIEF OF A BROOK TROUT ON TOP, CARVED FROM BASSWOOD AND DECORATED WITH GOATSKIN APPLIQUÉS AND INLAYS. IT CONTAINS A TWO-VOLUME SET OF TEXT AND A BOX WITH A SAMPLING OF EARLY FLY REELS, ALONG WITH DESIGNS THAT RENDER THE REELS ON THE COVERS. THE PROJECT TOOK MORE THAN TWO YEARS TO COMPLETE.

* * *

Left: LATE-19TH-CENTURY ENGLISH SALMON FLIES ARE EXHIBITED IN A MARBLED WOOD FRAME FROM THE SAME PERIOD.

Nor is it a surprise that museums and bibliophilic groups line up to witness, exhibit, and celebrate his one-of-a-kind creations.

"All the work has been created for my personal angling library," he declares of the hand-bound sets of fishing books, produced over a twelve-year period, that form the basis of a traveling exhibition, "The Collector as Bookbinder: The Piscatorial Bindings of S. A. Neff Jr.," which includes stops at the American Museum of Natural History in New York City and the American Museum of Fly Fishing in Manchester, Vermont. "In a sense," Neff observes, "the exhibition is the culmination of one angler's passion for fishing for trout with a fly."

In another sense, Sid Neff already had all the tools he needed to excel in his chosen new field when he first turned to bookbinding. After graduating from art school in 1960, he worked as a graphic designer for twenty-five years, including a stint as art director of *Trout,* the magazine of the conservationist organization Trout Unlimited. The experience gave him a well-developed aesthetic sense. His love affair with fly-fishing, which had begun when he was a teenager, imbued him with an angler's sensibility, one as rich and deep as any of the world's rivers he has fished. Even now, Neff fishes almost every evening in a stream near his home. The years of angling paid off in more tangible ways, too.

"I discovered that the hand-to-eye coordination and the patience I had developed in dressing trout flies were also useful in my efforts at binding," he reports. The veteran flytier had also finished scores of fly rods to his exacting standards, but, Neff concludes, "Building a rod was child's play compared to binding books."

Left: THE TRADITION OF BOOK-PLATES, WHICH BEGAN IN THE 18TH CENTURY, ENABLED THE SERIOUS COLLECTOR OF BOOKS, IN THE WORDS OF ONE, "TO AFFIX ON EACH RECRUIT SOME SPECIAL MARK OF OWNERSHIP BEFORE PASSING HIM TO THE RANK AND FILE OF HIS LIBRARY." PREVIOUSLY, NEW OWNERS OF A WORK WROTE THEIR NAMES DIRECTLY ON THE TITLE PAGE.

✳ ✳ ✳

Below: AMONG NEFF'S COLLEC-TION OF POSTCARDS ARE COMICAL REFRAINS ON THE STU-PENDOUS SIZE AND MULTITUDE OF THE FISHERMAN'S QUARRY.

✳ ✳ ✳

Opposite, below: A RARE COLLEC-TION OF SEVENTEEN WOODCUTS BY THE ENGLISH ENGRAVER JAMES MARCH INCLUDES SEVERAL THAT CAN BE MATCHED TO ILLUSTRA-TIONS IN BOOKS IN THE NEFF LIBRARY, SUCH AS THE WOODCUT *JACK, PERCH AND TROUT* IN *THE ANGLER'S GUIDE*, 1825, BY T. F. SALTER.

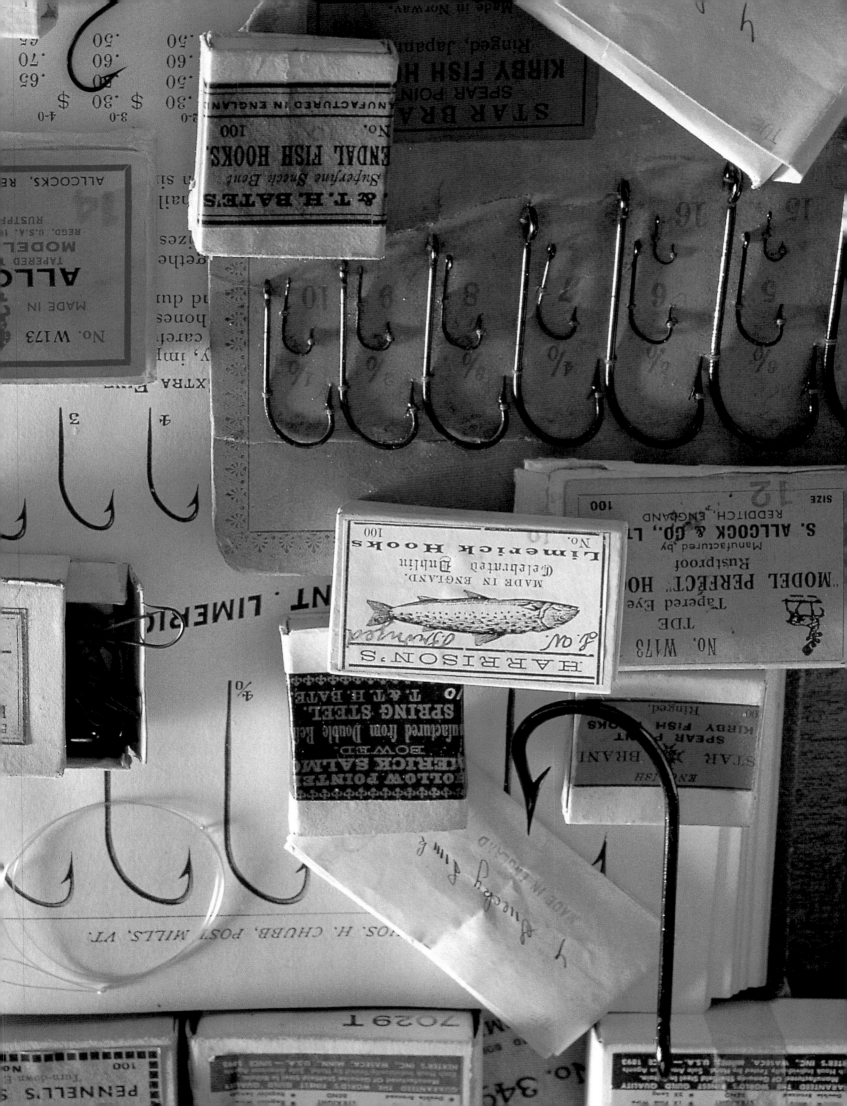

Opposite: NINETEENTH-CENTURY AND PRE–WORLD WAR II FLY HOOKS, SOME WITH EYES, SOME "BLIND," ALL IN THEIR ORIGINAL PACKAGING, ARE DISPLAYED AGAINST PAGES FROM THE FISHING EQUIPMENT CATALOG OF THOS. H. CHUBB, POST MILLS, VERMONT, PUBLISHED IN 1888.

* * *

Left: AN IRISH BROWN TROUT IS DEPICTED IN A BRILLIANT COLOR PLATE FROM A WORK AUTHORED BY THE RECTOR OF PRESTON-ON-THE-WEALD MOORS, SHROPSHIRE, ENGLAND, IN 1879.

* * *

Center left: GOVERNMENT-SPONSORED BROCHURES AND GUIDES, SUCH AS THESE CANADIAN TITLES FROM THE 1920S THROUGH THE 1950S, BECAME COMMONPLACE AFTER RAILWAY LINES OPENED UP VAST TRACTS OF THE NORTH AMERICAN WILDERNESS TO TRAVEL AND TOURISM.

* * *

Below left: ONE SECTION OF THE NEFF LIBRARY IS DEVOTED TO LATE-19TH- AND EARLY-20TH-CENTURY POPULAR BOOKS AIMED AT YOUNG SPORTSMEN, SUCH AS *FRANK THE YOUNG NATURALIST* AND *OAKDALE BOYS IN CAMP.*

* * *

Overleaf: ASPIRING TO CREATE "A KIND OF MINIATURE MUSEUM THAT ATTESTS TO AND SUPPORTS THE WRITTEN WORD," NEFF MADE THIS THREE-VOLUME SET, *MINIATURE NYMPHS,* TO ILLUSTRATE LIFE ON TWO TYPES OF TROUT RIVERS. IMAGES OF A BROWN TROUT IN A LIMESTONE RIVER, A RAINBOW TROUT IN A FREESTONE RIVER, AND THE INSECTS ON WHICH THE FISH FEED DECORATE THE BINDINGS.

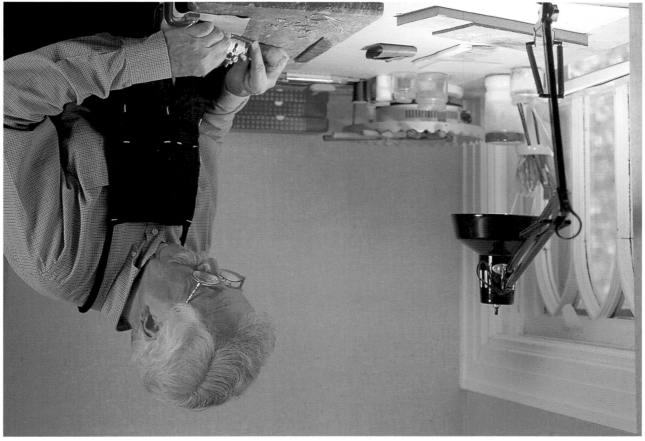

Opposite, above and below: SID NEFF'S BOOKBINDING STUDIO, A FLIGHT OF STAIRS UP FROM HIS LIBRARY, IS ALSO THE REPOSITORY FOR HIS "STABLE" OF FISHING RODS, HIS AUSTRIAN FISHING HATS BEDECKED WITH ANGLING BADGES AND MEDALLIONS, AND A WELL-STOCKED FLYTIER'S DESK.

* * *

Left: ARRAYED ON A FIELD OF AFRICAN GOATSKIN, THE TOOLS OF THE BOOKBINDER'S TRADE INCLUDE A FILLET, A WHEEL ON A LONG HANDLE THAT IS USED FOR TOOLING IN BLIND OR GILT; A ROUND-HANDLED IMPLEMENT OF NEFF'S OWN DESIGN, FOR BLIND AND GILT TOOLING; BONE FOLDERS, FOR FOLDING PAPER AND WORKING WITH LEATHER; A BROAD-CURVED FRENCH PARING KNIFE AND A SLENDER POINTED SWISS PAPER KNIFE; AND ENGLISH AND FRENCH GLUE BRUSHES.

* * *

Below: ROMANCE, A POPULAR THEME IN EARLY ANGLING POSTCARDS, IS INTRINSICALLY A PART OF NEFF'S PASSION FOR ANGLING AND FOR BOOKBINDING.

"To Draw with Leather"

In 1982, S. A. Neff Jr. set out to learn bookbinding simply to make repairs to old books he had collected. It took four or five years to master the basic technique and longer still for him to consider himself a master working in the centuries-old traditions of fine bookbinding yet embracing innovation with each new bookbinding project.

"Neff has continually added new methods, techniques, and materials to his bookbinding repertoire," notes Elisabeth Agro of Pittsburgh's Carnegie Museum of Art, in a catalog published in conjunction with a traveling exhibit of his work.

"I follow a direction dictated by the content of the text, the materials, and the tools," Sid says. For example, in blind tooling—a method of decorating a book in which impressions are made in the leather—he discovered the versatility of the Ascona tool, a specially cut brass tool that allows him to blind-tool impressions, using stiff paper templates of his own creation as a guide. This enables the binder to tool curvilinear lines more fluid than those made with conventional tools. "Sometimes the blind-tooled lines do not give enough definition to the design," he adds, "but I resolve this problem by gluing very narrow strips of goatskin, of a contrasting color, into the linear depression. This allows me to draw with leather."

Neff uses goatskins, originating in Botswana, Nigeria, and South Africa, which receive their necessary finish for his work in Scotland and France. Goatskin has a much longer life than sheep or calf and, when properly tanned, can last for almost a century.

In the late 1980s, Neff began working with Japanese dyed paper and gilt paper to create decorative panels for covers and doublures (the decoration on the inside of covers). "The process is begun by making a detailed drawing on tracing paper," he explains. "Colors are then selected from a chart of dyed-paper swatches. Next the images in the drawing are traced onto the dyed papers and cut out. They are glued to a piece of gilt paper and then put under a light weight to ensure that they dry evenly."

Later, each shape is carefully cut out, allowing a border of $1/16$ inch. When all the shapes have been prepared, they are glued in position on a piece of bristol board (a stiff acid-free paper made in several thicknesses), commencing with the sky and finishing with the foreground. By the time he has finished one image, Neff will have used several thousand pieces of Japanese paper and gilt paper.

"The process," Neff observes, "is not unlike assembling a puzzle."

Perhaps the most compelling innovation in Neff's work is his use of items such as actual fishing flies, photographs, letters, and reels, in addition to the decorative bindings, to convey the essence of the text of a book or essay.

"Almost from the start of my career," he states, "I have been intrigued with the concept of creating containers to house bindings and other volumes." Many of Neff's so-called containers take the form of a drop-back box covered with goatskin. All are decorated to various degrees, and this decoration generally sets a theme for the housed volumes.

"I am more inclined to call these box sets 'environments,'" notes Elisabeth Agro. "Each binding reflects his base of knowledge; each design is unique and particular to the subject of the book."

Above: TOOLS IN NEFF'S STUDIO INCLUDE A RED NIPPING PRESS FOR PRESSING BOOKS, AND A PLOW FOR TRIMMING EDGES OF A TEXT BLOCK. *Opposite:* A PANEL OF JAPANESE DYED AND GILT PAPERS DEPICTS AN IRISH BROWN TROUT IN THE LANDING NET, ONE OF MANY EXQUISITELY WROUGHT IMAGES IN *ANGLING IN HIBERNIA*, NEFF'S FIVE-VOLUME MEMOIR OF FISHING IN IRELAND.

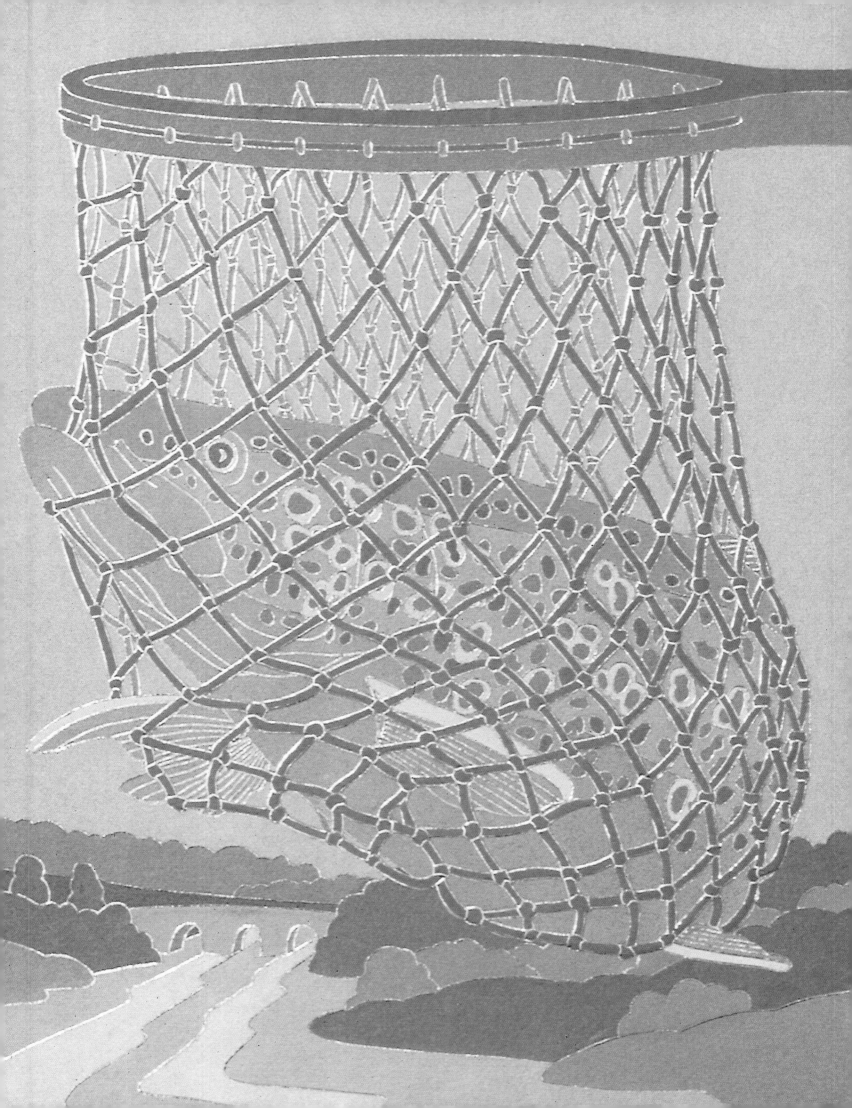

CLASSIC WATERING HOLE

A TOAST TO FISHING PIONEER ZANE GREY

BEFORE LUKE SHORT, Max Brand, Louis L'Amour, and a host of other popular adventure writers, there was Zane Grey. The dentist's son from Zanesville, Ohio, all but invented the genre of the western novel when he wrote *Riders of the Purple Sage* in 1912. In that classic story, a lone cowboy, the memorable Lassiter, leather-clad and packing two black-butted guns, metes out deadly justice to rustlers and kidnappers. Basing his vivid narratives

on his own travels in the intermountain West, Grey brought the romance and violence of the frontier to Americans hungry to know more about their vast continent.

Grey published a new western virtually every year for half a century; he was so prolific, in fact, that the publisher did not catch up with his manuscript production until two decades after the author's death in 1939. At the height of his fame, it was estimated that one-half of the entire United States population had read at least one of Zane Grey's works. More than 130 movies were made of his books. Even now, nearly a million copies of the westerns are sold each year throughout the world.

Yet for all his success as a novelist, Zane Grey was a fisherman at heart, and that spirit is captured in a mini-museum of Grey's life and career on display in a luxurious bar upstairs from World Wide Sportsman, an outfitter in Islamorada, Florida. The Zane Grey Lounge collection was acquired from the author's son Loren Grey by John L. Morris, owner of World Wide Sportsman

Opposite and inset: TALES OF THE ANGLER'S ELDORADO, ZANE GREY'S ACCOUNT OF FISHING IN THE WATERS OF NEW ZEALAND, WAS ONE OF A NUMBER OF BOOKS AND ARTICLES THAT HELPED TO POPULARIZE FISHING WITH LIGHT TACKLE IN THIS COUNTRY AND AROUND THE WORLD. HIS STORY ABOUT BONEFISH, PUBLISHED IN THE DECEMBER 1922 ISSUE OF *IZAAK WALTON MONTHLY*, INTRODUCED A THEN UNKNOWN GAME FISH TO THE WORLD. ANOTHER STORY, "RIVERS OF THE EVERGLADES," RECOUNTING A TARPON FISHING TRIP WITH HIS BROTHER, ROMER, CREATED A SURGE OF INTEREST IN TARPON.

* * *

Below: THE ZANE GREY LOUNGE IN ISLAMORADA, FLORIDA, WITH ITS COLLECTION OF THE AUTHOR'S FISHING GEAR, IS A FITTING TRIBUTE TO THE MAN WHO CELEBRATED AND IMPROVED UPON THE SALTWATER ANGLING TRADITIONS OF THE KEYS FROM HIS FIRST VISIT TO LONG KEY IN 1912.

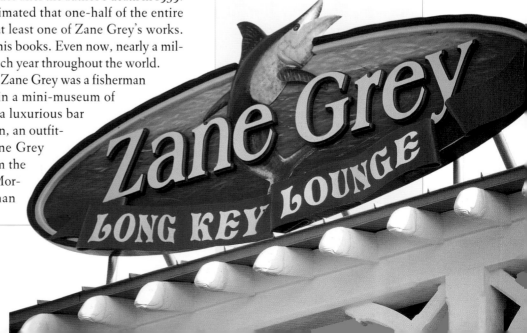

and president of Bass Pro Shops, the huge fishing equipment chain based in Springfield, Missouri.

The collection includes Zane Grey's most important books on fishing as well as four original manuscripts in his own hand, including "Big Game Fishing of New Zealand Waters." Tackle is on display, too, from a 3½-inch Hardy Zane Grey reel, one of only seven made circa 1930, to an 8½-inch Hardy Zane Grey reel made in 1932. (At one time, more than a dozen patented items of fishing gear were named after the writer.) A pioneer of light tackle, Grey stalked bonefish, "the wisest, shyest, wariest, strangest fish," as he called it, using what was known as three-six tackle, meaning a 3-ounce rod tip and 6-thread (18-pound test) line. Most bonefisherman of that era were using stiff rods with 36- to 45-pound test line.

Grey's first published story, in the May 1902 issue of *Recreation,* was an account of his fishing rivalry with his brother, Romer, and was titled "A Day on the Delaware." It was the westerns, however, that allowed him to fish all over the world, first in a 52-foot cruiser, *Gladiator,* then in a 119-foot three-masted schooner, the *Fisherman.* He fished for steelhead in the Rogue River of Oregon, tarpon off the coast of Nova Scotia and in the Gulf near Tampico, Mexico. He landed his first Pacific swordfish near Clemente Island, 36 miles from Catalina. At one time or another he held fourteen deep-sea fishing records. But he also knew what it felt like to be skunked—he once went eighty-three days of continual trolling off Papeete in Tahiti without catching a single fish.

The new home of the collection is highly appropriate because the Florida Keys were an important part of Zane Grey's fishing life. In 1916, he convinced railroad tycoon Henry Flagler that a construction camp Flagler operated on Long Key, not far from Islamorada, was ideal for conversion into an elite sportfishing lodge. The Long Boat Key Fishing Club was founded in 1916 with Grey as its first president. Located in a dense coconut grove at the western end of Long Key, the club compound consisted of a main lodge, fourteen cottages, and a post office and general store, with a marina and tackle shop on the bay side.

The club was well ahead of its time in its embrace of such causes as catch-and-release and the use of light tackle. When it published its membership book for the 1934–1935 season, it had entered into a full missionary mind-set, declaring as its goal "to become a power in the angling world, developing the best and finest traits of sport, to restrict the killing of fish, to educate the inexperienced by help, and shame the fish-hog by example, to teach the thing so imperatively needed in this country—conservation."

Alas, a greater power came along soon after and put an end to the club and its high-minded philosophy—the devastating Labor Day hurricane of 1935, with winds up to 200 miles per hour. Nothing of the camp was left standing.

"It is sad to think that Long Key, doomed by a hurricane, is gone forever," wrote Grey a few months later, "but that long white winding lonely shore of coral sand, and the green surf, and the blue Gulf Stream, will live in memory."

Left: ON THE MAIN FLOOR OF WORLD WIDE SPORTSMAN IS A BOAT OF SIMILAR VINTAGE TO THE FAMOUS *PILAR,* THE FISHING BOAT USED BY ERNEST HEMINGWAY IN CUBA AND STILL KEPT THERE. THE SISTER VESSEL WAS PURCHASED IN KEY WEST, PORTAGED TO SPRINGFIELD, MISSOURI, FOR RESTORATION, THEN BROUGHT BACK TO THE KEYS AND INSTALLED IN THE STORE IN ISLAMORADA.

* * *

Below: THE STORE'S CAST-BRONZE FLY ROD DOOR PULLS WERE DESIGNED BY TOM JOWETT AND MADE IN THE KEYS.

* * *

Bottom: MOLDED FISH GARGOYLES EXTEND FROM THE BUILDING'S RAFTERS IN THE IMAGE OF BONE-FISH AND RED FISH, ALSO DESIGNED BY JOWETT.

FANTASY FISHING ROOM

A COUNTRY HOTEL'S HOMAGE TO ANGLING

I THOUGHT ROOMS WERE for sleeping when it was too dark to fish," confesses angler John Ross in the preface to *North America's Greatest Fishing Lodges*. But in the course of profiling more than 250 upscale lodges for the guidebook, Ross was disabused of that notion by his partner and collaborator, Katie Anders—not the first fisherman to discover more of the niceties of life from a discerning female.

For Anders, a former senior editor at *Country Inns* magazine, he relates, "'upscale' meant more. Her mind sees rooms decorated with quality furnishings and coordinated fabrics, plus amenities."

By those lights, Twin Farms, the award-winning country hotel in Barnard, Vermont, is not just upscale but off the scale, and nowhere is its deep-seated luxury and playful elegance more evident than in the cottage called The Perch. A carved salmon looms large over an inviting bed set back in a paneled alcove, separated from the main room by a hand-carved arch of wooden roping. A whimsical metal fish, fashioned from a commercial sign found in Brooklyn, oversees the large copper bathing tub in its own windowed alcove in the bathroom. Elsewhere, The Perch is graced with antique fish decoys and carvings, old artifacts such as ice-fishing spears, and contemporary art that adds a whimsical dimension to the world of angling.

Copper Lake, a 7-acre pond on the property, is stocked with rainbow trout, some of them solid 24-inchers,

Opposite and left: OF ALL THE ACCOMMODATIONS AT TWIN FARMS, THE PERCH COTTAGE IS THE MOST TRADITIONALLY ENGLISH, WITH A SPORTING TWIST. FROM THE DRESSING ROOM, WITH ITS TROPICAL-FISH MURAL BY BOYD REAPH STUDIOS, NEW YORK, ONE GLIMPSES A MAIN ROOM ADORNED WITH WOOD AND METAL SILHOUETTES AND CARVINGS OF GAME FISH.

* * *

Below: HOLLY LANE'S MIXED MEDIUM PICTURE *HAVING NO EYELIDS, THEIR EYES ALWAYS LOOKED STARTLED* IS ONE OF SEVERAL FISH-RELATED IMAGES DESIGNED TO MAKE PERCH GUESTS SCRATCH THEIR HEADS AND PERHAPS SMILE.

Top right: BATHROOM TILES WERE CUSTOM DESIGNED FOR TWIN FARMS BY ARCHITECT SCOT CORNELIUS.

* * *

Center right: ARCHITECT ALAN WANZENBERG DESIGNED EIGHT FREE-STANDING COTTAGES OF WOOD AND STONE, INCLUDING THE PERCH, FOR TWIN FARMS, WHILE DESIGNER JED JOHNSON WAS RESPONSIBLE FOR FURNISH-ING AND DECORATING EACH COT-TAGE IN A STYLE ALL ITS OWN.

* * *

Bottom right: AN ANGLING THEME QUIETLY INFORMS THE FIREPLACE IN THE PERCH, BEGINNING WITH ITS ANDIRONS.

* * *

Below: A FISH WAS FASHIONED OUT OF A COMMERCIAL SIGN FROM BROOKLYN BY ARTIST RICHARD BAKER.

* * *

Opposite: WITH A CARVED AND PAINTED SALMON OVER IT, THIS BED HOLDS OUT THE PROMISE OF DEEP COMFORT FOR ANY ANGLER WHO HAS FISHED THE DAY AWAY.

reports Greg Newton of Blue Ridge Outfitters in Chittenden County, Vermont, who is available to school Twin Farms guests in fly-fishing on the pond or in the nearby White River, "not well known but one of the state's better fishing rivers, especially in the deep holes by the numerous iron bridges that span it." Newton grew up on a farm in Vermont and worked for Orvis, the tackle company based in Manchester, Vermont, before starting his own guide service. "I've been fly-fishing since I was eleven," he notes, "and I pride myself on helping beginners get the hang of it. If they will stand for four hours of instruction on the pond in the morning, I'll have them catching fish on the stream in the afternoon."

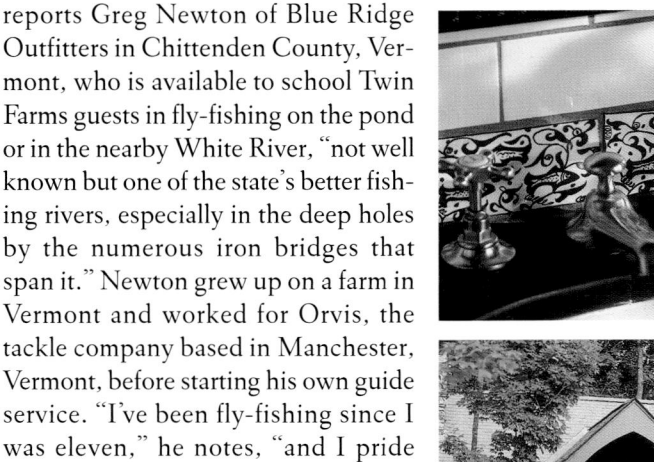

Twin Farms, which opened in 1993, has a history of warm country hospitality dating back to the 1920s, when the original 1795 farmhouse was acquired by Sinclair Lewis, America's first Nobel Prize–winning author, and his wife, the pioneering female journalist Dorothy Thompson. The two threw lavish parties for the literary set of the day, including H. L. Mencken, Rebecca West, and J. Vincent Sheean. Thompson called the place "the best expression of life for both of us—beautiful, comfortable, hospitable, and unpretentious," and, many years later, it measured up to that standard again after a multimillion-dollar makeover. In 1974, the property was bought as a vacation home by the Twigg-Smith family of Honolulu, Hawaii, descendants of the missionaries Asa and Lucy Thurston, who first brought Christianity to the islands in 1820. Thurston Twigg-Smith, the present head of family, ran a vast newspaper empire in Honolulu prior to the acquisition. Avid contemporary art and folk art collectors, the Twigg-Smiths lent many pieces from their private collections (they founded the Contemporary Museum of Art in Honolulu) to decorate Twin Farms. They commissioned architect Alan Wanzenberg and designer Jed Johnson to refurbish the main house and barn and build eight freestanding cottages of wood and stone throughout the 300-acre property.

With so many creature comforts available, including a world-class restaurant and wine cellar, guests at Twin Farms may be forgiven for opting for a sedentary stay here. But just in case, Copper Lake, its canoes, and its state-of-the-art Orvis tackle are provided for the pleasure of guests. Then it's back to The Perch for a satisfying soak in the copper tub at day's end, under the friendly gaze of a metal fish from Brooklyn.

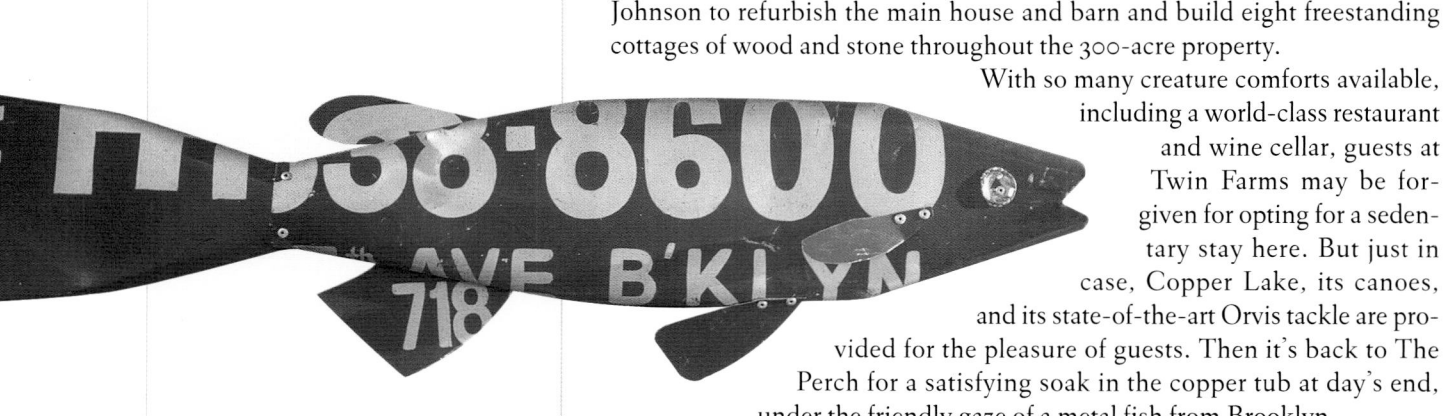

AMERICA'S ANGLING ARCHIVES

BACKSTAGE AT THE MUSEUM OF FLY FISHING

IT IS THE ultimate fisherman's attic, crammed with all the things that anglers accumulate over a lifetime, only in volume, literally—volumes and volumes of fishing titles dating back to 1700; thousands of rods, reels, and flies; shelves and shelves of pictures, prints, etchings, posters, catalogs, periodicals, and brochures; boxes filled with leather fly wallets and tackle boxes; and a host of curiosities of slight historic interest, such as Bing Crosby's pipe, General George S. Patton's creel, and early American rod maker Hiram Leonard's flute, mentioned by Henry Thoreau in his writings.

It is the collection of the American Museum of Fly Fishing, located in a sweetly unassuming white clapboard building in historic Manchester Village, Vermont. This gem of a small museum has organized some of its materials into engaging and informative exhibits on the main floor of the building, but the side rooms and upper story give the full effect of the collection.

"Fly-fishing is built on its traditions and artifacts," noted Nick Lyons in his keynote address on the occasion of the twenty-fifth anniversary of the museum, which was founded in 1968. "There is a subtle and seamless web that joins all life in the waters we fish and there is an equally complex web of relationships in the life and spirit and mores of those who protect them." He added, "Our unique museum plays an indispensable role in keeping that vanishing past vividly, momentously, alive. It is our anchor and our heart, and our memory."

Opposite and below: THE TROUT AND SALMON FLIES OF MARY ORVIS MARBURY ARE PERHAPS THE MOST HISTORIC FLIES IN THE MANCHESTER, VERMONT, MUSEUM'S COLLECTION. MARY WAS BORN IN 1856, THE SAME YEAR HER FATHER, CHARLES, STARTED THE COMPANY THAT BECAME FAMOUS FOR PROVIDING AFFORDABLE RODS, REELS, AND FINELY TIED FLIES TO A MUSHROOMING POPULATION OF ANGLERS. AT THE AGE OF TWENTY, MARY WAS PUT IN CHARGE OF THE ORVIS COMPANY'S FLY-TYING DEPARTMENT. BY 1890, SHE AND A HALF-DOZEN YOUNG WOMAN TIERS WERE PRODUCING UNTOLD QUANTITIES OF EACH OF THE MORE THAN 400 DIFFERENT PATTERNS LISTED IN THE ORVIS CATALOG.

Right: A PAINTING BY CATHERINE
M. WOOD IN 1890, DEPICTING FIVE
FLIES TIED IN THE AREA OF
ABERDEEN, SCOTLAND, SHOWS
THE FLAMBOYANT USE OF COLOR
THAT WAS COMMON IN FLY TYING
IN THE VICTORIAN ERA.

* * *

Below: NOT ONLY IS THE AMERI-
CAN MUSEUM OF FLY FISHING
AND THE HISTORIC AMERICAN
FLY-FISHING OUTFITTER, ORVIS,
FOUND IN MANCHESTER, VER-
MONT, BUT SO IS THE BATTENKILL
RIVER, ONE OF NEW ENGLAND'S
MOST FAMOUS TROUT STREAMS, A
PERENNIAL DESTINATION OF FLY
FISHERS FAR AND WIDE.

Pages 76–77: PINS FROM FISHING
CLUBS, CAMPS, AND OTHER
ANGLING ORGANIZATIONS ARE
DEPLOYED ON AN EARLY
LEATHER-BOUND EQUIPMENT
CATALOG FROM ORVIS.

The museum was born from the marriage of a singular idea—lifelong angler Hermann Kessler's idea—and a relatively small assortment of memorabilia stored in the old Orvis factory building in Manchester. (Charles F. Orvis started his fishing tackle company in 1856 and it soon grew into a prosperous mail-order business selling rods, reels, and flies.) To make the collection more comprehensive, appeals went out to magazines and newsletters, and donations started coming in almost immediately.

"In that first year," reports a museum aide, "twenty-one rods, ten reels, artwork, and some miscellaneous tackle was received," as well as Herbert Hoover's fishing gear, "the first components of our ever-growing personality-statesmen collection."

Year after year, more donations flowed in from members, from friends, and through word of mouth. Some gifts were collections in themselves: over 1,000 flies tied by E. R. Hewitt, William Cushner's framed flies, Frederic Sharf's 250 antique reels, Theodore Gordon's fishing books. The widow of Michigan Supreme Court Justice John D. Voelker donated the fishing effects of her husband in 1991. Voelker, who wrote *Trout Madness* and other fishing

classics (as well as the best-seller and Oscar-winning movie *Anatomy of a Murder*) under the pen name Robert Traver, is represented at the museum by his Orvis Impregnated Limestone Special rod, a box for his Italian cigars, and a battered enamel fishing cup that accompanied him on his fishing outings, nestled in a market basket on the seat of his Jeep, along with bourbon, bottle opener, jigger, and water, according to his wife.

Other singular donations included Charles Ritz's Tyrolean hat, festooned with pins of fishing clubs the world over; a stained-glass window depicting a fishing scene; and President and Mrs. Carter's fishing rods. Before long it became necessary for the museum to hire a full-time curator. Its library alone had swelled to more than 3,000 books.

"Fly-fishing is more than mere sport," says executive director Gary Tanner. "It is art, craft, history, tradition, ethics, philosophy, literature, geography, industry, biology, and conservation all rolled into one passionate pursuit. And we at the museum strive to shed light on fly-fishing in all its many dimensions."

Left: THE CENTRAL IMAGE OF THE MUSEUM'S EXHIBIT ON AMERICAN FLY REELS IS THE 1888 PORTRAIT OF HIRAM L. LEONARD, ROD BUILDER AND REEL MAKER OF BANGOR, MAINE, PAINTED BY HIS WIFE, ELIZABETH. "THE LEONARD RAISED-PILLAR REEL HAS LONG BEEN A FAVORITE OF ANGLERS," WRITES JIM BROWN IN HIS MONOGRAPH ON THE MUSEUM'S FLY REEL COLLECTION, *A TREA-SURY OF REELS.* "ITS SOUND CONSTRUCTION AND CLASSY GOOD LOOKS, ALONG WITH THE MAGIC OF THE LEONARD NAME, ALSO HAVE MADE IT HIGHLY PRIZED BY COLLECTORS."

Top: "THE HAND THAT WIELDS THE ROD RULES THE REEL," READS THE COPY IN AN EARLY TACKLE CATALOG, EXTOLLING AN ALUMINUM REEL THAT REQUIRED ONLY THE ANGLER'S LITTLE FINGER TO MAINTAIN CONTROL OF HIS LINE.

* * *

Above: THE BOY SCOUTS OF AMER-ICA ENDORSED A FLY-TYING KIT TO GET MORE BOYS ON THE STREAM IN THE 1950S; SINCE THEN, ALMOST AS MANY FEMALES AS MALES HAVE TAKEN AN INTER-EST IN FLY-FISHING AND ITS RELATED SKILLS AND PRACTICES.

Top: AT THE MUSEUM'S ANNUAL OPEN HOUSE WEEKEND, VISITORS GET THE CHANCE TO MEET FLY-TIERS, ROD MAKERS, AND OTHER ARTISTS AND ARTISANS OF THE SPORT OF FLY-FISHING.

* * *

Center: IN A COLLECTION THAT SPANS NEARLY TWO CENTURIES OF BRITISH AND AMERICAN REEL MAKING, FLY REELS OWNED BY PRESIDENTS, ENTERTAINERS, NOVELISTS, AND ANGLING LUMINARIES SIT SIDE BY SIDE WITH REELS OWNED AND USED BY EVERYDAY ANGLERS. IN ADDITION TO SOME 1,200 REELS, THE MUSEUM HAS MORE THAN 1,100 FLY RODS AND UPWARDS OF 25,000 TROUT AND SALMON FLIES IN ITS ARCHIVES.

* * *

Bottom: PERMANENT EXHIBITS DRAW ON THE MUSEUM'S EXTENSIVE COLLECTION OF TACKLE AS WELL AS PHOTOGRAPHS, ART, PRINTED BOOKS, MANUSCRIPTS, AND RELATED MATERIALS. A TRAVELING EXHIBIT, "ANGLERS ALL," BRINGS SOME OF THE MUSEUM'S RICHES TO THE PUBLIC ON STOPS ACROSS AMERICA.

* * *

Opposite: THE WELL-ORGANIZED STACKS IN THE BACK ROOMS OF THE MUSEUM OF FLY FISHING ATTEST TO THE DEPTH AND QUALITY OF THE COLLECTION, MOST OF IT DONATED BY FLY FISHERMEN DEVOTED TO MAINTAINING THE STANDARDS AND VALUES OF THEIR SPORT.

BESPECKLED
TROUT
EST.1993

CATCH OF THE DAY

DINING IN PISCATORIAL STYLE

WHEN OUR PEOPLE come in for lunch out of the helter-skelter of the city, they feel like they're on a trout stream in the country for an hour and a half," says Don Rapino, the manager of Anglers & Writers, a popular neighborhood restaurant in the West Village section of New York City, which one reviewer has called "a refreshing oasis in a fast-paced city that shouldn't be missed."

Diners who tuck into the generous portions on the American farm food menu here find themselves surrounded by Leonard and Thomas cane rods, hand-tied fishing flies, old landing nets, tackle boxes, early-edition fishing books, and inspirational fish carvings and paintings. The eatery and the candy store next door, Bespeckled Trout, with its own unique angling-cum-confections decor, are the brainchildren of Craig Bero, an actor-turned-restaurateur from the wilds of northern Wisconsin.

"It looks like a little fishing lodge but it's in the middle of Manhattan," notes Bero. Craig modeled the restaurant, which opened in 1990, after the general store his grandfather owned and operated when he was growing up in Algoma, a small town on Lake Michigan, an hour's drive northeast of Green Bay. The tin ceiling in the restaurant came from Wisconsin, as did the milled white ash lumber used for its flooring. Bero obtained the oak bar from an old fishing lodge in Nicolet National Forest in his home state.

When Bero first contemplated opening a restaurant, he knew he wanted it to reflect him and the things he liked to do. Not only has he fished since the age of four, but he has spent a lifetime scouring flea markets and estate sales for fishing memorabilia. His restaurant and candy store constitute a shrine to the angling milieu in which he grew up.

"My grandfather's store was a place where fishermen gathered to trade stories," Bero recalls, "and I would listen to their fishing talk every day. I remember studying their hands, which were gnarled and weather-beaten. Yet their eyes were always incredible pools of blue. I firmly believe this came from life near the water." He adds, "Someday I'd like to have that poetry in my own eyes."

Top and right: THE RESTAURANT
WAS PATTERNED AFTER ONE OF
NORTHERN WISCONSIN'S TYPICAL
FISHING LODGES, WITH CANE
RODS AND CARVED AND PAINTED
FISH ON THE WALLS, CREELS AND
LANDING NETS IN THE CORNERS,
AND OLD ANGLING BOOKS AT
HAND FOR BROWSING.

* * *

Above: THERE IS NO CREEL LIMIT
ON THE CHOCOLATE TROUT
AVAILABLE IN THE CANDY SHOP
NEXT DOOR TO THE RESTAURANT.

* * *

Opposite, above and below: WHILE
BESPECKLED TROUT ENTICES
VISITORS WITH A SWEET TOOTH,
ANGLERS & WRITERS RESTAURANT
BECKONS WITH A MENU OF
FARM-STYLE FARE AND A
HANDFUL OF RAVE REVIEWS.

2
AT THE LAKE

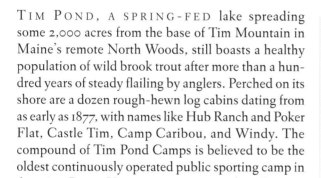

TIM POND, A SPRING-FED lake spreading some 2,000 acres from the base of Tim Mountain in Maine's remote North Woods, still boasts a healthy population of wild brook trout after more than a hundred years of steady flailing by anglers. Perched on its shore are a dozen rough-hewn log cabins dating from as early as 1877, with names like Hub Ranch and Poker Flat, Castle Tim, Camp Caribou, and Windy. The compound of Tim Pond Camps is believed to be the oldest continuously operated public sporting camp in America. In pre-Victorian times, sports from Boston, New York, and Philadelphia made the journey here by train, stagecoach, and buckboard to enjoy the fantastic fishing on the lake —it was not uncommon for early anglers to catch 20 pounds of fish a day —and to experience a fortnight of comfortable wilderness living (camp meals served at 7:00 A.M., noon, and 5:00 P.M., with guests summoned by horn from the front steps of the dining hall). A century later, guests were still showing up, and so were the fish, admittedly only about 9 to 10 inches long, and rarely weighing more than 2 pounds, but still handsome, healthy, and feisty.

Tim Pond may epitomize the enduring appeal of life on a wilderness lake, but there is also plenty of good,

even great, fishing to be had on quiet farm ponds, old mill ponds, steep-sided mountain lakes at the higher altitudes, and the country's multitude of man-made lakes.

People who have never fished are often astonished to learn of the range and complexity of fishing habitats. Warm-water lakes are the most numerous bodies of still water in the United States, but they fish differently depending on the depth and clarity of the water and the time of day and time of year. And if they are resort lakes with cigar boats and personal watercraft roaring across the surface, they might not fish at all: the noise drives fish into cover. (The *silence* of fly-fishing, of course, is what draws more meditative outdoorsmen to the sport.) Another warm-water habitat has come into being in a big way with the development of man-made lake systems and impoundments, which crafty bass fishermen scout with electronic depth finders and by consulting detailed maps showing features of the land before it was inundated.

Mountain lakes, being so much higher and subject to colder temperatures, also vary enormously in terms of angling opportunities. Deep, clear-water lakes with rich underwater weed growth in their coves and bays tend to be good producers of fish populations.

> **THERE IS AN**
>
> · · · · · · · · · · · ·
>
> **ABIDING**
>
> · · · · · · · · · · · ·
>
> **PLEASURE IN**
>
> · · · · · · · · · · · ·
>
> **HAVING A LAKE**
>
> · · · · · · · · · · · ·
>
> **ALL TO YOURSELF.**
>
> · · · · · · · · · · · ·
>
> —*Larry Koller*

Opposite: AN INFORMAL PICTURE JOURNAL OF THE TRAVELS OF BARNEY, SUSAN, AND ERIN ESTRELLE BELLINGER COMMUNICATES ONE FAMILY'S ZEST FOR FISHING AND CANOEING THE LAKES OF THE ADIRONDACKS. THE BELLINGERS, WHO MAKE RUSTIC FURNISHINGS, NAMED THEIR WORKSHOP SAMPSON BOG STUDIO AFTER A POND IN ADIRONDACK PARK, WHERE, SAYS BARNEY, "OUR FAMILY HAS TAKEN MORE THAN A FEW JOYFUL TROUT FISHING EXCURSIONS."

According to Larry Koller, author of *The Treasury of Angling*, the most significant feature of the mountain lake is that its waters divide into three distinct temperature zones in the summer months. So if you are fishing for cold-water species such as salmon, trout, and smallmouth bass, don't expect to find them in the top 15 or 20 feet of water—the lake's upper layer will be too warm for them. Another cold-water habitat, the famous ten thousand lakes of Minnesota and almost as many in neighboring Wisconsin, provide ideal breeding conditions for the premier game fish of northern waters in the Midwest, northern pike and muskellunge (nicknamed "muskie").

And then there are the Great Lakes themselves. America's five mammoth freshwater seas, stretching across eight states from Minnesota to New York, abound in lake trout, brown trout, walleyes, smallmouth bass, muskies, northern pike, king salmon, and many more species. Lake Erie alone is estimated to accommodate a population of 64 million fish, a remarkable fact for a body of water once so polluted that it literally caught on fire from time to time. (Besides conservation efforts to reduce oil spills, the arrival of the nonnative

zebra mussel reportedly did much to filter and clarify Lake Erie's waters.) Great Lakes anglers troll for fish from boats, surf-cast from the shore, or fish from the innumerable piers and jetties that stick out from shore into the lake's watery domain.

Even the humble farm pond, if it is endowed with rich plant life, can be a prodigious breeder of bass or pickerel, panfish such as perch, crappies, and bluegills, or bottom-feeding catfish. Easy to fish from a bank or from a small boat or raft brought to within casting distance of the weedy growth along shore, farm ponds provide a microcosm of the light-tackle fishing experience. "The farm pond is hardly a treasure for the polished and sophisticated angler," writes Charles F. Waterman in *The Fisherman's World,* "although he sees there the problems of angling in concentrated form, applicable in varied scale to a thousand other situations where the end result may be steelhead or a sailfish."

Many of these locales resist and in some cases forbid human settlement. Anglers come and go in such places, but generally do not raise a permanent roof over their heads. In others, though, fishermen have put down roots and established outposts in a tradition and style

Above: LIKE MANY OF THE LAKES IN THE ADIRONDACKS, BLUE MOUNTAIN LAKE WAS FIRST SETTLED IN THE LATE NINETEENTH CENTURY, WITH HOTELS AND LODGES OF MODEST TO GRAND SCALE CROPPING UP IN THE WAKE OF THE EXPANDING RAILWAY SYSTEM. CITY DWELLERS CAME FOR THE CRISP MOUNTAIN AIR, ANGLERS FOR THE PRODIGIOUS NATIVE FISH POPULATIONS, AND SOME VISITORS STAYED ON AND BUILT CAMPS AND COTTAGES OF THEIR OWN.

that date back to the era when the Tim Pond Camps in Maine were built.

"Keeping in mind that humans first lived in caves and huts for thousands of generations," observes Ralph Kylloe in *Fishing Camps,* "the owners of these new retreats kept tradition with our ancestors by decorating in the style of their forebears. This style included trophies of the hunt, artwork of the animals that were fished and hunted, fishing and hunting tools, fireplaces, and furniture made of natural materials such as antlers, logs, sticks, and roots."

In fact, some of the cabins at Tim Pond still boast the original fireplaces, iron beds, makeshift tables, and wicker rockers, according to Spence Conley, who wrote about the old camp in *The American Fly Fisher.* There are messages from the past scratched into the log walls of the cabins. There are bottles buried on the camp common as time capsules, a summer tradition dating from the 1920s, filled with news reports of the day, letters, poems, and other personal messages. Today, says Conley, no one can remember where the time capsules were buried.

In some ways, the best part of a retreat on the lake or in the woods or at the shore or on the mountain is that it represents time in a bottle for those who have had the good fortune to experience its seductive privileges. On a call-in radio show, the art critic for a major daily newspaper unhesitatingly describes a porch overlooking Lake Erie, where he whiled away countless summer hours as a child, as "the most important room in my life." Likewise, a man shows a friend the battered canoe he salvaged from an old camp on Lake Ontario before the camp passed out of his family's hands not long ago. The boat won't float and it clutters up his garage, but it is a reminder of the man's childhood, and perhaps it even stands for the identity of his lost youth and better self.

Memory's idealizing habit, of course, cannot obscure the fact that, in a world of homelessness, the second home is quite a perk, and second-home syndrome, like a marriage arranged between blue-blood cousins, is a mechanism for keeping the rest of the world out. Wilderness retreats provide respite from city life and from the barbarian other. Yet "the wildness and adventure that are in fishing still recommend it to me," as Thoreau said, in *Walden,* and so long as anglers respect those twin facets of their passion, who is to say they are not entitled to enjoy and perpetuate their lordly lean-tos and palaces of pine?

Above: STU DAVIDSON WETS A LINE IN BERKELEY LAKE, A TINY SPRING-FED LAKE NEAR ATLANTA, GEORGIA, WHILE HIS SIX-YEAR-OLD AKITA, BUDDY, KEEPS AN EYE OUT FOR MORE APPETIZING SPORT. *Overleaf:* EVERY SPRING, STU AND HIS WIFE, LINDA, RUN A BASS TOURNAMENT ON THE LAKE FOR FRIENDS AND NEIGHBORS, COMPLETE WITH MODEST CASH PRIZES FOR THE BIGGEST CATCHES OF THE DAY.

FISHING FOR LIFE

ALL FOR ART, FRIENDS, AND FAMILY

SCOTT ZUCKERMAN was on a ladder, painting a 10-foot-long sign on front of the Housatonic Meadows Fly Shop, not far from his home in Connecticut, when a car with California license plates came to a screeching halt on the roadside.

"That's the most beautiful painting I ever saw!" exclaimed the driver, jumping out of the car. There he stood for a minute, staring up in obvious admiration at the image on the sign, a trout rising to a mayfly—a familiar moment of epiphany for expert anglers on the Housatonic River every spring. Then he got back in the car and sped off before Scott could thank him for his nice words.

Properly speaking, Zuckerman is an artist specializing in sporting themes, not a sign painter, but he is not averse to an occasional paying job in the world of commerce, especially if it is conveniently in the neighborhood. "As long as I have a brush in my hand," he says, "I would do it."

In fact, one of the artist's heroes is Woody Guthrie, who was a sign painter himself before hitting his stride as a singer and writer of songs with a strong social bent. Zuckerman also has compassion for the working bloke, having been mentored by two of that ilk when he was still young and in search of himself in the early 1970s in Southwest Harbor, Maine.

One was an aging boat painter who led "a kind of stumblebum existence," according to Zuckerman, yet was possessed of a talent that was much in demand by wealthy yacht owners. Once the man was hired to paint the stripes along the gunwale of a 44-foot Hinckley—the gold standard in yachting at that time. Scott found him sleeping off a night on the town under another boat in the yard and managed to get him to his assignment.

"It was the most incredible feat of virtuosity I ever saw," Zuckerman recalls. "He picked up his brush and ran two perfect pinstripes down the length of the boat, exactly an inch apart, and his hand never wavered."

The more important influence at this juncture, however, was Wendell Gilley, a plumber by trade who eventually gained fame for his hobby, bird carving. By the time Scott met him, Gilley had been carving wood likenesses of nearly every North American bird species in every scale for more than forty years, and it would not be long before his work was recognized for its artistic merit with a special exhibit at the Academy of Natural Sciences of Philadelphia. Today, there is a museum of decorative bird carvings in his name in Southwest Harbor.

When he first met Gilley, Scott had been working for a commercial art firm, turning out six or seven landscapes a day, "pretty much clichés of waves crashing on rocks and lobster traps pitted with age," he admits. "Wendell Gilley took one look at my work and told me to paint birds, fish, and animals instead."

His apprenticeship to Gilley extended beyond helping the craftsman add a painted surface to his carved birds, Zuckerman says. "We went fishing and hunting together, and I learned a lot about the woods from him. He taught me taxidermy, which he himself had learned from a correspondence course. A lot of his Maine independence and sensibility rubbed off on me. At night I'd watch him sit by his Franklin stove, carving birds. If he didn't like the way one was shaping up, he'd throw it in the fire, and I admired

Opposite: WITH SOME MINIMAL INSTRUCTION FROM HER FATHER, JAIME ZUCKERMAN BECAME AN EXPERT FLYTIER AT AN EARLY AGE, AND STILL FASHIONS TROUT FLIES FOR THE FAMILY'S USE. HER YOUNGER SISTER, BRITTANY, HAD NO INTEREST IN THE CRAFT BUT LOVES TO FISH WITH THE FLIES THAT JAIME MAKES.

Above: MANY OF THE FLIES TIED BY JAIME ZUCKERMAN FIND THEIR WAY INTO HER FATHER'S WORKING COLLECTION OF FISHING LURES.

* * *

Right: THE COUPLE'S BEDSIDE TABLE SAGS UNDER THE WEIGHT OF BOOKS AND PERIODICALS, MOST OF THEM RELATED TO ANGLING. THE RAINBOW TROUT WAS PAINTED BY SCOTT WHEN HE WAS EXPERIMENTING WITH THE RICH, DARK-TONED PALETTE OF THE OLD MASTERS.

Left: GUN CASE, BOOKCASE, AND TABLESCAPES OF THE SPORTING LIFE INFORM THE ZUCKERMAN LIVING ROOM WITH VESTIGES OF THE WILD. THE BRONZE OF A EUROPEAN BROWN BEAR ON THE TABLE DATES FROM THE LATE EIGHTEENTH CENTURY AND WAS MADE BY ANTOINE LOUIS BAYRE, CONSIDERED ONE OF THE GREAT ANIMAL SCULPTORS, WHO WAS ALSO THE TEACHER OF RODIN.

* * *

Below: WHEN SCOTT'S FRIEND J. AUSTIN FORBES PRESENTED HIM WITH A MINIATURE GRAPHITE AND CORK FLY ROD HE HAD MADE, THE ARTIST TESTED IT SUCCESS- FULLY ON A NEARBY POND. ON A ROD AS SMALL AS THIS, A TINY PANFISH ACQUIRES THE FIGHTING CHARACTERISTICS OF A MIGHTY TROUT OR SALMON.

* * *

Bottom: ZUCKERMAN SPENDS FROM SIX TO TEN HOURS A DAY IN HIS STUDIO, SEVEN DAYS A WEEK, "WHEN HE IS REALLY COOKING" AND WHEN THE LURE OF THE WOODS IS NOT TOO STRONG.

Above: A SEPARATE BUILDING NEAR THE HOMESTEAD HOUSES SCOTT'S PAINTING STUDIO, SCATTERED WITH TACKLE HE HAS FOUND AT TAG SALES AND FLEA MARKETS, SUCH AS LURES, RODS, REELS, AND FISH HOOKS STILL IN THEIR ORIGINAL PACKAGING, IMAGES OF ANY OF WHICH MAY FIND THEMSELVES IN ONE OF SCOTT'S CREATIONS SOMEDAY. THE FISH OVER THE DRAFTING TABLE BY THE WINDOW IS A PICKEREL THAT THE ARTIST LANDED IN NEARBY STONY BATTER POND.

* * *

Opposite: SCOTT ZUCKERMAN'S FISHING VEST SHOWS OFF HIS MEMBERSHIP BUTTON FOR THE SHARON, CONNECTICUT, FISH & GAME CLUB, A LOCAL SPORTING GROUP WITH 60 MEMBERS, 100 ACRES OF FARMLAND, AND A STOCKED 10-MILE RIVER.

that. He carved because he enjoyed it, not just to obtain a result. The joy was in the doing."

By the time Scott moved to the foothills of the Berkshires in 1979 with wife Joanne and daughters Jaime and Britt, he had become a painter in his own right, with gallery representation in Manhattan (the esteemed J. N. Bartfield Galleries, whose strong suit is the western paintings of Frederic Remington and Charles Marion Russell). Scott also has assorted other supporters and corporate clients with deep pockets, including one that commissioned two hundred paintings.

"If you want something bad enough," Zuckerman says, reflecting perhaps the stoic convictions of his blue-collar mentors from Maine, "the world will conspire to help you get it," and that includes his family's two-hundred-year-old house with its four more recent add-ons, which sits on 50 wooded acres populated by wild things of every kind.

Scott grew up saltwater fishing in Port Washington, New York, where he made "the monthly pilgrimage to the drugstore to pick up *Field & Stream, Outdoor Life,* and *Sports Afield,*" no copy of which he has ever thrown out. Family camping trips in New England introduced him to freshwater fishing, and he continues that tradition on the Housatonic, along streams that wander through his own property, and in nearby Stony Batter Pond.

Ever the optimist, Zuckerman "made it a point to go fishing every day to ground myself" following a heart attack and corrective surgery in June of 1999 "for arteries so blocked you couldn't have gotten a fish line through them." The event, he said, "like the old saying about imminent hanging, brought clarity of thought. I stopped smoking, made my diet healthier, and just began to really appreciate life. I got a lot of paintings done. It turned out to be a wonderful summer."

WOVEN WONDERS

IN SEARCH OF VINTAGE FISHING CREELS

THE FLY FISHERS' outfit, to be complete, requires the creel for the reception of the fish caught," wrote a certain Dr. Charles T. Mitchel in the December 1892 issue of the *American Angler.*

Brian Correll, whose love of angling and basketry first led him to collect fishing creels, can't argue with the good doctor's prescription, which is why his house at the edge of the Adirondack Park in New York is brimming with of creels of all kinds—some handmade by Indians or Shakers, others produced on the assembly line in China or Korea, still others turned out by itinerant workers with the honesty and flair of folk artists.

"Creels, in fact, are great pieces of folk art," Brian asserts, at least the older and best crafted of them, which today fetch prices in the thousands of dollars at auction. Basically, they are baskets with lids with holes in them, originally used to hold the fisherman's catch as he continued to cast into streams for salmon or trout. With the popularization of catch-and-release policies for those species, the utilitarian value of the creel declined, "although you still see some people using them," Brian notes, and he does see them, even at a distance of 200 yards while cruising along at 50 or 60 miles per hour.

"I was driving on a highway next to the St. Lawrence River in Canada when I saw this guy fishing for salmon with a beautiful leathered creel over his shoulder," Brian relates. "I jammed on the brakes, turned around, parked, got out of the car, and made my way down to the river. It turned out the fisherman spoke only French. I could tell the creel had probably been in his family for a couple of generations. I pointed at it and made signs I was willing to give him money for it, but he had no intention of letting it go."

Correll, whose name is almost an anagram of the object of his desire, began fishing when he was growing up in East Stroudsburg, Pennsylvania, a mostly rural area where angling is still a way of life for many citizens, and got off to a particularly auspicious start.

"I was only four when my dad signed

Opposite: A GRAIN-PAINTED CABINET FROM THE MID-19TH CENTURY IS FILLED WITH A WIDE VARIETY OF HANDMADE AND FACTORY-MADE CREELS, INCLUDING IMPORTS FROM CHINA AND KOREA. THE MIDDLE CREEL ON THE TOP SHELF WAS MADE TO BE USED BY A CHILD ANGLER. ONE OF BRIAN CORRELL'S PERSONAL FAVORITES IS THE BARREL-SHAPED CREEL ON THE RIGHT, SECOND SHELF FROM THE TOP.

* * *

Left: A CREEL MADE FROM CIGAR BOXES IN THE LATE 19TH CENTURY SITS ATOP A YELLOW BIRCH CHAIR MADE BY RENOWNED ADIRONDACK CRAFTSMAN LEE FOUNTAIN IN THE 1920S OR 1930S.

* * *

Below: THE 6-POUND 2-OUNCE, 2-FOOT-LONG BROOK TROUT WAS CAUGHT ON HORSESHOE LAKE IN LABRADOR. LEATHER-STRAPPED CREELS DATE FROM THE 1940S OR '50S.

me up for a local fishing tournament on a small nearby stream," he recalls. "He set me up by the stream and I threw my worm in a hole. Moments later something was pulling on it. Actually, I dropped the rod when I saw the fish, then grabbed the fish with two hands and threw it up on the bank where I pounced on it. It was about an eighteen-inch rainbow and won first prize!"

Creels were made in England and elsewhere in Europe in the eighteenth century, but the craft flourished when it emigrated to the New World. Native American tribes in the woodlands of Maine, upstate New York, and the Midwest developed the classic split-creel checkerwork and birch-bark creels, while Indians of the Pacific Northwest made beautifully woven and decorated creels. Although most of these creels were made for trade with American and European anglers, it did not take long for discerning collectors to elevate these baskets to a form of art, especially those which had been berry-stained with delicate images of trees and wildlife.

For anglers looking for a portable container to hold their catch, basketry creels, lightweight and able to flush water that got into them, were a vast improvement over the canvas and leather carryalls of the day, which quickly became waterlogged on the stream. The early creels were fashioned from long narrow strips of ash, willow, or oak. Machine-cut splints replaced the hand-cut variety after 1880. At almost the same time, a machine was developed to harvest willow as a uniform caning material, and willow creels soon went into heavy commercial production.

Early in this century, saddle and harness manufacturers began to produce creels with leather trim for the growing sporting marketplace. Oregon was a hotbed of this activity, with several firms specializing in making sturdy creels in a variety of styles. The George Lawrence Company and W. H. McMonies & Company, both of Portland, produced the top-shelf creels of the era and were among the few makers to place their name on each of their creels.

THE RUSTIC LEGACY

EPITOME OF WILDERNESS STYLE

SINCE AROUND 1900, it had served as a boys' camp, a girls' camp, a music camp, a religious camp, and just about every other brand of summer camp. Even today, the three-story rustic barn building of Larch Lodge, with its spacious open plan and numerous landings, has the air of an idyllic summer retreat where there is much to do and plenty of time to do it in. In fact, Bert and Nancy Savage still get people knocking on the door who were campers here back in the 1920s, '30s, or '40s, "and they are quick to point out exactly where they slept," says Bert.

Located in New Hampshire's wooded highlands east of Concord, the lodge serves both as the Savages' home and as a fitting showcase for the antique rustic furniture and accessories that Bert has specialized in collecting since the early 1980s. In the 1960s and 1970s he had established a reputation as a dealer in fine Early American furniture. The place is also home to Colwyn, the kennel name under which Bert has bred, trained, and shown champion Welsh terriers since 1949.

Rustic furnishings are much in demand today compared with the days when Bert started out in the field, "when Early American antiques shows would not even permit you to show a rustic piece," he relates, "and most designers hated it because it took them too much time and effort to locate for a client." For a time, following World War II, a lot of rustic ended up in dumps and landfills, he says,

Opposite: THE BED, CHEST, AND DRESSER, OF YELLOW BIRCH WITH WHITE BIRCH BARK, WERE ORIGINALLY MADE FOR A NORTHERN NEW HAMPSHIRE GIRLS' CAMP IN ABOUT 1920. FLANKING THE ARTS AND CRAFTS LAMP ARE ELECTRIFIED TIGER CONCH SHELLS, MADE IN THE 1920S TO SERVE AS NIGHT-LIGHTS.

Above: THE FISH MOUNT, MADE TO DUPLICATE THE SIZE, COLORATION, AND OTHER FEATURES OF A FISH CAUGHT BY A VISITING ANGLER, WAS CARVED BY LAWRENCE C. IRVINE OF WINTHROP, MAINE.

* * *

Left: BERT SAVAGE'S DAUGHTER-IN-LAW, SHARI, MADE THE LODGE SIGN IN ITS EMBRACE OF ELK ANTLERS.

"because people just preferred aluminum lawn chairs with plastic webbing." The revival of interest in rustic came with the booming economy of the 1990s and the rapid growth in the second-home market. "Unlike the fishing camps of old, which were used only a couple of months a year and so were furnished largely with low-end furniture and other hand-me-downs," Bert observes, "today's vacation homes are furnished and equipped for year-round enjoyment, so the taste level has risen, even though the desire for a casual, no-fuss lifestyle is still there."

This market places a premium on the one-of-a-kind rustic works that Bert enjoys tracking down, like the elaborate twig veneer desk made in the 1920s by Charles Albert Sumner, who was the caretaker of Birch Point Camps in the Rangeley Lakes area in Maine for many years, or the fish mounts of another Down Easter, Lawrence C. Irvine. Irvine's works are the carved and painted likenesses of actual fish caught and mounted on handmade cutouts of the state of Maine. Paintings of trout and salmon are also of high interest, as are the store samples of canoes that were made in the 1920s by companies like Peterborough Boats or Old Town Canoe. Unlike more mundane icons of the wilderness, such as wooden skis, rawhide snowshoes, or sap buckets, these small replicas of canoes were made with the same high craftsmanship of the finished products from those manufacturers, and they make an elegant addition to a contemporary river, lake, or mountain house.

Above: THE CABINET WITH SHAKER TABLE TAILORING WAS MADE IN ABOUT 1937 BY THE OLD HICKORY FURNITURE COMPANY. LIKE THE WINDSOR-STYLE CHAIRS FROM THE SAME PERIOD, IT WAS FOUND IN AN OLD MINNESOTA FISHING CAMP. THE BIRCH-BARK AND TWIG MIRROR WAS PROBABLY MADE IN THE ADIRONDACKS IN THE LATE 19TH CENTURY.

* * *

Below: SOUVENIR PADDLES FROM THE THOUSAND ISLANDS AREA OF THE UNITED STATES AND CANADA DATE FROM THE 1920S AND MEMORIALIZE SUCH SUMMER RITUALS AS "A SHORE DINNER."

Old summer camps are still a source of some of the things that Bert deals in, but he points out that camps for girls tend to yield more noteworthy pieces than camps for boys. "Historically," he observes dryly, "young male campers have been hard on furniture." Yet only recently he managed to convert a sow's ear into a silk purse. "I picked up twelve or thirteen armchairs from one camp that looked as if they had been used by the campers to throw a party to end all parties. Not one chair was without major damage. But they were made by the Old Hickory Furniture Company of Martinsville, Indiana, in the 1920s, so they were classics well worth trying to rescue. [Old Hickory made the furniture for many of the cabins and lodges in America's national parks, including the Old Faithful Inn in Yellowstone Park, where the tables and chairs are still in use.] By cannibalizing one chair to fix another, we ended up with nine perfect Old Hickory armchairs."

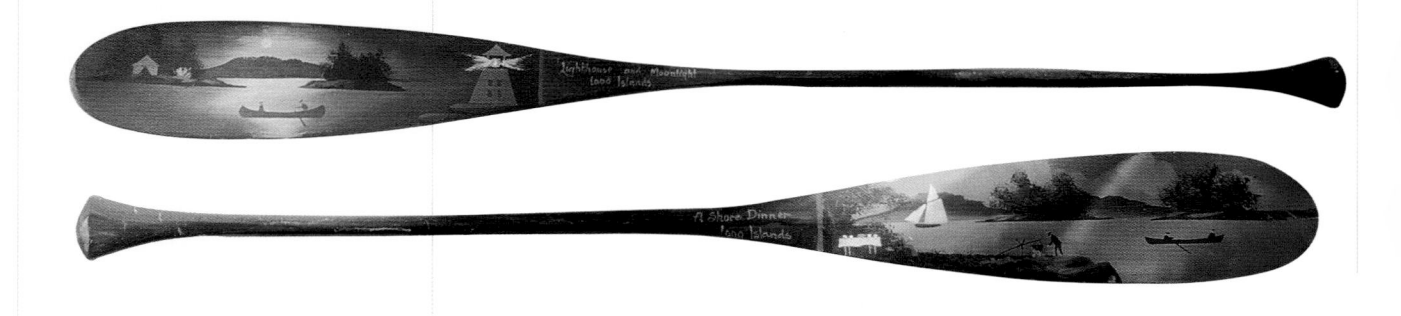

Left: FISH TROPHIES HAVE BEEN
MOUNTED ON BOARDS IN THE
SHAPE OF MAINE, CARVED BY
LAWRENCE C. IRVINE. THE
BIG BASS, WEIGHING IN AT
6 POUNDS 8 OUNCES, WAS
CAUGHT BY BILL RANDALL ON
ANNABESSACOOK LAKE IN MAINE
IN 1973. MEMENTOS ON THE DESK
INCLUDE A PHOTO OF WILLY, ONE
OF BERT AND NANCY SAVAGE'S
CHAMPION WELSH TERRIERS.

* * *

Below: NANCY SAVAGE STARTED
COLLECTING DECORATED SHELL
PIECES AS A LARK IN THE 1960S.
GATHERED FROM AS FAR AWAY AS
THE SOUTH PACIFIC, THE EXOTIC
SHELLS WERE OFTEN TAKEN
NORTH AND DECORATED FOR THE
TOURIST TRADE WITH IMAGES OR
INSPIRATIONAL MESSAGES LIKE
THE LORD'S PRAYER. *LEAPING
TROUT,* IN THE BACKGROUND, IS
AN OIL ON BOARD, CIRCA 1900.

"Bigger, Better, and Barkier"

Beginning in the first years of the twentieth century, the tables, chairs, and other furnishings of the Old Hickory Furniture Company of Indiana were sold in great numbers—an estimated 2,000 pieces a week at the peak of the company's seventy-year existence—in department and furniture stores all over the country.

Hickory, plentiful in Indiana, lent itself to factory production, but as Craig Gilborn, former director of the Adirondack Museum, asserts, the best rustic furniture of that era was the one-of-a-kind handiwork of the guides, loggers, and carpenters who came into their own in the Adirondacks in the 1880s and 1890s with the building of the great camps, such as Topridge, Pine Knot, Kamp Kill Kare, and Uncas, and the dozens of smaller camps and cabins that sprang up on the vast holdings of the Adirondack League Club. Today, a new generation of furniture makers and other craftspeople are producing pieces of exceptional quality and originality for the latest wave of wealthy settlers in the wild. "Some are from old money, others made it less than an hour ago," observes Ann Stillman O'Leary in *Adirondack Style*. "Nonethless, the competition for bigger, better, and barkier is on—and it is a spectacle to behold."

Rustic furniture style is not uniquely the product of the Adirondacks, however; rather, it is a style of many regional facets, influenced by the conditions, traditions, and materials found in different areas. In the Appalachian South, willow, rhododendron, and moun-

tain laurel became the raw materials of folk arts and country crafts. In Florida lengths of red cypress and driftwood found their way into chairs, tables, and settees. In the West, cabins and ranches of lodgepole pine are likely to reverberate with cowboy art, Native American beads, baskets, and blankets, and the fanciful furniture of Thomas Molesworth, complete with burls and decorated with antlers. In California is found an ever-changing, always eclectic style that borrows from Spain, Mexico, Asia, and Hollywood.

A hooked rug at Bert Savage's Larch Lodge illustrates the appeal of the rustic vision. Made in upstate New York in the 1920s, its figural components include a lake, a bluebird, a campfire, and a moose—all icons of the imagined good life in the wild, brought together in a simple rug that approaches folk art. "Like almost all the good ones," Bert observes, "this rug will surely go on the wall."

"Each region has its own vernacular of furnishings and architecture," states Ralph Kylloe, an expert on rustic style who represents some of the best living rustic artisans through his Lake George, New York, gallery. He maintains that rustic style's universal appeal lies in its implicit promise of connection to the natural world. "People respond to rustic style and want to live surrounded by it because we are all in reality part of nature," he says. "We used to live in huts and caves, and that is hard-wired into our brains. That's why we go to lakes and rivers, why we keep dogs and cats near us, and why we have plants in the house."

Rather than approach rustic style in an academic fashion, Kylloe encourages people to create and compose their rustic settings from their own instincts. "Decorating in the rustic style is fun, and most of us do not need to hire decorators to do what we know by instinct," he asserts. "In us all are the secret messages of nature. We all hear the call. It is from whence we came."

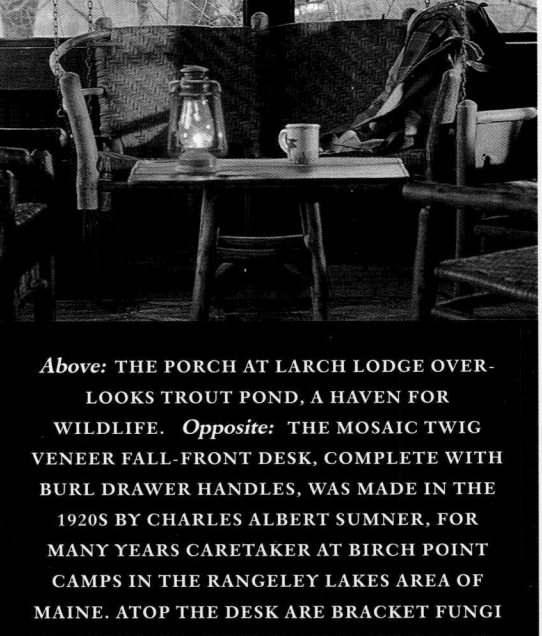

Above: THE PORCH AT LARCH LODGE OVERLOOKS TROUT POND, A HAVEN FOR WILDLIFE. *Opposite:* THE MOSAIC TWIG VENEER FALL-FRONT DESK, COMPLETE WITH BURL DRAWER HANDLES, WAS MADE IN THE 1920S BY CHARLES ALBERT SUMNER, FOR MANY YEARS CARETAKER AT BIRCH POINT CAMPS IN THE RANGELEY LAKES AREA OF MAINE. ATOP THE DESK ARE BRACKET FUNGI THAT WERE HARVESTED FROM TREES A HUNDRED YEARS AGO, THEN PAINTED.

ICE CAPADES

FISHING FOR GLORY ON ASHFIELD POND

LATE IN FEBRUARY every year, on a Saturday morning, as many as eighty or ninety kids turn out for the Ashfield Rod and Gun Club's annual ice-fishing derby on Ashfield Lake. Old maps of this hill town in western Massachusetts actually identify the body of water as a pond, but there's still plenty of room for the youngsters, in some cases joined by a parent, to deploy across the exhilarating blue-white expanse, with plenty of space left over for freelance hockey players and wandering dogs.

By this time of year, a foot or more of solid ice usually has formed on top of the lake, 12 inches being the minimum thickness deemed necessary to safely entertain the pink-cheeked, parka-clad hordes, and the absence of oxygen in the light-starved bottom layers of the water has driven fish to the shallows. There are pickerel and bass to be had, and panfish like perch and bluegills, but just to be sure there will be lively angling, the club has also stocked the lake with a couple hundred trout obtained from a private fish hatchery.

"We want to give kids the experience of fishing through the ice," says Russell Williams, club secretary for the past decade. Founded in 1920, the club is one of thousands that sprang up in that era when declines in wildlife populations made it clear that sports like hunting and fishing required a good dose of self-regulation. Youth education is an ongoing goal of the 200-member Ashfield club. "Our derby introduces young people to a positive activity at a time of inactivity, in our northern climate, and it also shows them how to prepare for being out in cold weather. We give out twenty-five prizes, including a $25 gift certificate

for the largest fish [this year, a 24-inch pickerel]. If you get cold, you can always go into the Lake House [a friendly lakeside eatery] for hot drinks and food. Some kids take to ice-fishing, others don't, but the event is always lots of fun."

Rituals like the derby are repeated in one form or another on lakes and ponds all across the

Opposite: MOTOR-DRIVEN ICE
AUGERS HAVE TAKEN THE WORK
OUT OF CREATING A FISHING
HOLE IN THE ICE. BAITED,
THE TIP-UP RIG ALERTS THE
FISHERMAN WHEN THERE'S A
BITE ON THE LINE.

✳ ✳ ✳

Below: FOR THE ASHFIELD DERBY,
THE BAIT OF CHOICE WAS FRESH
MINNOWS FROM SILVER PANTHER
BAIT & TACKLE.

✳ ✳ ✳

Bottom: ARRAYED AGAINST AN
EARLY AMERICAN CABINET FROM
UPSTATE NEW YORK ARE FISH AND
EEL SPEARS, OR GIGS, DATING
FROM ABOUT 1800 TO THE 1940S,
AN ADIRONDACK GUIDE'S
LEATHER MAP CASE, TIE-UPS FOR
ICE-FISHING, AND A HANDMADE
SPLINT CREEL OF UNUSUALLY
LARGE SIZE, CIRCA 1870.

northland every winter. Ice-fishing is a cult practiced by people who are actually cheered by the prospect of below-zero nights and cold, gray days. Their professional attire consists of "adding enough clothing until your arms stick out at 45-degree angles," says outdoor writer Bob Knopf, who ice-fishes on Spirit Lake, Iowa, "and thick earmuffs so you don't hear the ice crack as you walk about."

On Mille Lacs in central Minnesota, some 5,000 devotees erect ice-fishing houses every winter, some complete with carpeting, bunkbeds, and TV. The local Jaycees give away $100,000 in ice-fishing prizes. The state's love affair with ice-fishing was the backdrop for some of the funnier scenes in the movie *Grumpy Old Men,* starring Jack Lemmon and Walter Matthau. But the film could just as easily have been shot on Lake Winnipesaukee in New Hampshire, on Holmes Lake, a snowball's throw from Lincoln, Nebraska, or on any number of urban reservoirs in Colorado.

Although many practitioners have turned ice-fishing into a high-tech sport, with the use of gas-powered augers (to drill holes in the ice), portable shelters, and electronic fish finders, the children of Ashfield are content to fish with jigging poles, which look like a mini rod and reel with a hook, sinker, and small bob attached to it, or with tie-ups, self-standing fishing devices that signal when a fish is on. Bait, conveniently for sale at the Silver Panther Bait & Tackle Shop, next to the Lake House, consists of meal worms, live minnows, and night crawlers.

In its simplicity, this approach resembles the ancient Native American practice of ice-fishing with spears and fish decoys. Instead of shanties, picture tepees all over the lakes, the native angler within, prone on pine boughs by the hole in the ice, his spear at hand, a wooden carving with a white belly and lead-filled cavity and glass eye at the end of the jigging stick, bobbing in the viscous green water.

Today, fishing with spears is restricted by regulation, but it was once an important subsistence activity for the tribes of the northland. Ironically, ice-spearfishing was adopted by white rural dwellers during the Depression also as a means of putting food on the table in winter, yet it inadvertently led to a bonanza for well-heeled angling collectors to come.

During the revival of what was called the poor man's sport in the 1920s and 1930s, hundreds upon hundreds of fish decoys were carved with consummate skill out of basswood, white pine, or tulipwood by such midwestern artisans as Oscar Peterson, Hans Janner Sr., and Pecore Fox. Originally made and sold to support the craftsman and his family, fish decoys have since risen to the heady status of folk art, with monetary values attached to them that would have staggered the original makers. Organizations have sprung up solely devoted to preserving and promoting the fish decoy as collectible Americana folk art.

"We collect what we like," write Art and Scott Kimball, co-editors of a newsletter published by the American Fish Decoy Association. "Fish that 'smile at us' are the ones we keep."

WELCOME TO OUR LAKE

A COUPLE'S BASS-FISHING RETREAT IN GEORGIA

LINDA DAVIDSON of American Antiques was beaming. She'd just gotten off the phone with a fellow dealer in Florida who had tabs on a rustic place with fabulous lighting that was going out of business near Clearwater Beach. Such leads help antiques dealers like Davidson keep their inventory fresh by uncovering new sources for materials. In this case, the dealer reported that the business, Moon Lake Lodge, had gnarly 5-foot-long cypress knees hanging from the ceiling, all aglow with appliance bulbs. Linda snapped them up at once.

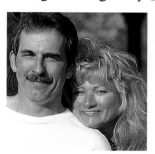

"Don't you think they'll be great in our living room?" she enthuses. "The lights will look just like stars overhead!"

Linda and her husband, Stu, seldom pause in their efforts to keep fresh and starry-eyed the sporting ambience of their house on Berkeley Lake outside of Atlanta, Georgia. Ever since moving here fifteen years ago, the couple has in effect been following the pronouncement of William S. Wicks: "The modern representative of city life must not dream of going into the woods and living like a savage."

So Wicks wrote in his 1889 classic, *Log Cabins and Cottages: How to Build and Furnish Them.* The MIT-trained architect was a pioneer in promoting the use of natural logs as legitimate building materials for residences in this country, and his treatise became, as Elizabeth Folwell observed in *Adirondack Life,* "the little book that launched a trend."

In the same spirit as Wicks's vision of rustic country life, Linda and Stu set forth to civilize the humble three-room cabin, complete with leaking roof, that was built in 1957 by the son of a minor league baseball manager. The Davidsons replaced the outdated sunroom with a dining room and installed vaulted ceilings. Deck, boathouse, and var-

Opposite and left: A MOUNTED PAIR OF DEER, THE DOE WEARING A MINNIE PEARL HAT, AND A SAUCY EMBOSSED PHOTO OF A NUDE ON LEOPARD SKIN, DATING FROM ABOUT 1910, SET THE TONE FOR THE MASTER BEDROOM OF LINDA AND STU DAVIDSON. AN ARTS AND CRAFTS–STYLE NEWEL-POST BED HAS BRASS ROSETTES, PINE CONE–LIKE SPINDLES, AND A VICTORIAN BRASS CHAIN STRUNG FROM POLE TO POLE.

* * *

Below: LINDA DAVIDSON HAD THE CARVED MOOSE ON THE BOATHOUSE MADE FOR HER HUSBAND AS A SURPRISE, THEN INCORPORATED A PAIR OF WEATHER-BEATEN CANOE PADDLES IN THE FINISHED PIECE.

Above: WITH ITS EXPANSIVE VIEW OF THE LAKE, THE MAIN ROOM OFFERS A CHOICE OF PLUSH SEATING, INCLUDING AN OLD HICKORY COMPANY GLIDER FROM THE 1930S, COVERED WITH AWNING-STRIPE LINEN AND A BEARSKIN RUG.

* * *

Preceding pages: BERKELEY LAKE OUTSIDE OF ATLANTA, GEORGIA, IS THE VENUE FOR STU DAVIDSON'S ANNUAL BASS TOURNEY, A FRIENDS-AND-NEIGHBORS RITUAL OF SPRING THAT TAKES PLACE RAIN OR SHINE.

nished wood-ribbed canoe soon followed. Linda, who makes frequent buying trips for her home-based business, brings back whatever her heart tells her to.

"Anything that brings the outdoors in, that can give a place the feeling you get in a mountain cabin or an old Adirondack lodge, is what I'm attracted to," she says. "I also look for old farm-made things, like picture frames and lamps —those one-of-a-kind objects that were made for a certain purpose."

Almost all her life Linda has been a lady of the lake. She grew up in Cleveland, Ohio, 2 miles from Lake Erie. During high school, she spent weekends at a lake house in Indiana belonging to the family of a girlfriend whose mother collected antiques and inspired Linda to take an interest in them as well. Her own father, an avid sportsman, would take the family on summer trips to Stoney Lake, north of Toronto, Canada.

Linda's husband, a computer programmer in Atlanta's bustling high-tech marketplace, likes fishing so much that he organized a bass tournament for their neighbors on the spring-fed 86-acre lake back in 1992, and it has grown into an annual fixture on Berkeley Lake's spring social calendar. Most years, thirty or more local anglers turn out in their bass boats and canoes, and they manage to catch and release more than one hundred fish. Only artificial lures and plastic worms may be used, and the bass must be at least 12 inches long to be accepted at the weigh-in, which is held on Stu's dock at the end of the day. There are prizes for the biggest fish and the heaviest stringers of three fish. One year Stu himself captured the prize for the biggest fish by catching a large-mouth bass that tilted the scales at 3 pounds 12 ounces

"It was a little embarrassing to win my own tournament," says Stu, "but it was a good fish."

Left: THE "WELCOME WOODMEN"
PENNANTS IN THE GUEST
QUARTERS WERE MADE BY LINDA
FROM OLD ARMY BLANKETS,
IMPRINTING THE DESIGN WITH
WOOD BLOCKS AND OCHER OIL
PAINT. THE MOOSE PILLOW ON
THE BED WAS MADE BY A FRIEND,
ROWANN SANDERS, ALSO FROM
ARMY-BLANKET MATERIAL. THE
POT-METAL CLOCK LAMP WITH
THE ANGLER FIGURE ON IT IS
DESIGNED SO THAT THE FISHING
ROD MOVES UP AND DOWN WITH
THE MOVEMENT OF THE CLOCK
AND, WHEN IT FUNCTIONS AS A
NIGHT-LIGHT, A FISH SILHOUETTE
SHOWS UP FLOATING IN THE
TANK. THE STITCHERY PORTRAIT
OF A COTTAGE ON A LAKE WAS
MADE IN THE 1930S.

Above: THE DINING AREA BOASTS
A 6-FOOT OVAL OAK TABLE
MADE BY THE OLD HICKORY
FURNITURE COMPANY IN 1915.

✳ ✳ ✳

Overleaf: SELECTIONS FROM
LINDA'S COLLECTION OF POST-
CARDS, SEVERAL SHOE BOXES'
WORTH; AND A WALL VIGNETTE
OF FISH, DEER, AND A PRINT OF
A KINGFISHER FROM THE
EARLY 1920S.

ADIRONDACK VISION

IN THE FRAMEWORK OF FISH

BARNEY BELLINGER named his furniture workshop and studio in Mayfield, New York, after a small lake in the West Canada wilderness area of the Adirondack Park. It's a 9-mile carry over rough terrain just to get to Sampson Bog, but the artist makes several camping trips there a year, sometimes alone, sometimes with family and friends, to fish, to canoe, to soak in the sights and sensations of the wild.

"Early one spring morning, when the mist was still coming off the water," he recounts, "I was in my canoe no more than 20 feet from the shore when a black bear and her two cubs appeared. I was upwind from them, so the mother didn't pick up my scent, and I was able to watch her methodically search for breakfast for the family, turning over rocks and logs."

The grandson of a logger, Bellinger grew up with a profound appreciation of the romance and mystery of the Adirondacks, its camps and logging trails, its wildlife refuges and secluded fly-fishing sites, and its rugged mountains and dense, lush woods. "I cherished the time my grandfather spent with me when I was a child, fishing and sharing the secrets of the woods," he says. "He would talk about white pine, spruce, hemlock, alder, and yellow birch as though they were old friends, which in a sense they were."

Today, Barney's intimate knowledge of the life of the woods allows him to transform "the chaotic, windblown, twisting, and rain-battered contours of wood" into custom-designed tables, beds, wall shelves, cabinets, and fly-fishing desks. "The most important influence on our furniture is our respect for nature and our love of fishing and of the outdoors," he adds.

Often harvesting for materials by toboggan in winter, he searches out blow-down areas of the

BUNTING & EMERY CO.   FRESH FISH

forest for extraordinary root and tree base configurations that have potential to become unusual bases for pedestal tables. He also looks for the glow of the yellow birch, variegated in color from gold amber to siena chocolate tones; they create antique finishes with mosiac patterns on the furniture. A single twig mosaic on a larger piece such as a cabinet might contain as many as 1,300 pieces.

The work of Sampson Bog Studio is inextricably bound up with the cycles of nature. "We know when the sap has started and stopped running—if it's timely to harvest a tree for reshaping into a tabletop, and how to preserve that wood," says Bellinger. "Understanding the sap flow is crucial—only if the tree is cut at the right moment will its bark adhere to it in the years to come." What nature sloughs off, Barney and his wife, Susan, exploit. "Neighbors who know we make furniture often bring us antlers that they've collected after deer shed them in late winter," Barney reports, "and my daughter Erin enjoys searching for the acorns and pine cones that Susan uses on many pieces."

When Barney incorporates an oil painting into one of his pieces—as the centerpiece on a headboard, say—the result, to some observers, bears comparison with the work of the noted Adirondacks painter, Levi Wells Prentice, or even Winslow Homer. Delicately hued, the landscapes are miniature oval windows onto the vastness of the wild.

And yet Bellinger is completely self-taught. He did paint for a living for two decades—he painted motorcycles and automobiles, that is—and he carved commercial signs with gold leaf and fancy fretwork ornamentation. Bellinger credits his professional transformation to a chance visit he and Susan made to the Adirondack Museum in Blue Mountain Lake in 1990. Overwhelmed by the beauty and craftsmanship of the early rustic furniture on exhibit, fashioned by loggers and guides of another era, he was seized with the idea of making furniture in that tradition. "I was especially impressed with the works of Ernest Stowe and Lee Fountain," says Barney. Stowe was a bachelor carpenter who produced rustic furniture for camps on the Saranac Lakes around the turn of the century. He worked mostly with unbarked yellow birch and panels of white-birch bark, fashioning desks, bookcases, and sideboards with classical lines and proportions. Lee Fountain, who for years ran a hotel in Speculator, New York, and later a general store, was a prolific maker of rustic chairs and tables in the 1910s and 1920s. "From their pieces, we got an idea to make furniture that respected the earliest traditions of Adirondack craftsmanship, yet were a little different."

A few short years later, with a waiting list of clients almost as long as the carry to Sampson Bog, Barney could fairly declare, "My lifetime of respectful devotion to the gifts of the forest has become a vocation."

Opposite: BELLINGER MADE THE BOOKCASE OUT OF AN OLD DUCK BOAT FROM THE 1920S, ORIGINALLY FOR USE AS A TRADE SHOW DISPLAY CASE, BUT HE LIKED IT SO MUCH HE MOVED IT INTO HIS LIVING ROOM. IN ITS RUSTIC FRAME, THE CALENDAR FROM 1917 TAKES ON A TIMELESS APPEAL, AS DOES THE PICTURE OF ANGLERS BY PHILIP GOODWIN, WHO PAINTED SPORTING SCENES FOR COMMERCIAL PATRONS OF THE ERA.

Above, clockwise from left: BARNEY BELLINGER AT THE ADIRONDACK ANTIQUES SHOW; A 20-INCH BROOK TROUT CAUGHT BY THE ARTIST AND INSTALLED IN "AN ANGLER'S COLLAGE REPRESENTING THE FLY FISHER AND THE BIRCH-BARK OUTDOORS"; AND EIGHT-YEAR-OLD ERIN BELLINGER'S CEDAR RIVER CREEK CLUBHOUSE, TEMPORARILY CLOSED DUE TO SCHOOL.

* * *

Overleaf: INSIDE SAMPSON BOG STUDIO.

FISH OUT OF WATER

ADIRONDACK MUSEUM ANTIQUES SHOW

CANOE PADDLES were going for $95, early black-and-white photos of fishing camp geezers for $30 and up. Joe Fionda of Male Antique Decor had a Hardy Brothers fly wallet from the 1920s priced at $1,285 and stuffed to the gills with English fishing flies. Bert Savage was offering a pair of oil paintings from Maine of trout (Ram Island) and landlocked salmon (Sebago Lake) by one J. Mead, circa 1900, in their original frames, for $3,900. Ross Brothers, the specialist in early boats, canoes, and skiffs out of Florence, Massachusetts, had a colorful bunch of lures, circa 1940, from the Marathon Bait Company of Wausau, Wisconsin. Somebody was even trying to sell a full-sized stuffed moose for $1,200.

Welcome to the annual Adirondack Museum Antiques Show, held on the museum grounds in Blue Mountain Lake, New York, a one-day gathering of some of the finest, and most bizarre, rustic art, furniture, and accessories in the country, and all for sale. Started in 1992 primarily to increase awareness of the museum, "the best museum of its kind in the world," according to the *New York Times,* the antiques show has grown into an event that inspires superlatives of its own.

"Honestly, when we went into it, we weren't even sure it was going to fly, but that first year we had 52 exhibitors and 2,200 visitors," reports Jerry Oliver, whose management company, Oliver and Gannon Associates, has handled the show since its inception. "It has grown every year. In less than a decade we had more than doubled the number of exhibitors and nearly tripled the gate."

The show has also sparked considerable satellite activity, with exhibitors springing up on the street all the way to Indian Lake. Some are dealers who were unable to get space on the show grounds; others are local residents who've

Left: CANOES, GUIDE BOATS, AND MAMMOTH MOOSE ANTLERS ARE EMBLEMS OF THE ADIRONDACK EXPERIENCE WITH ALMOST TRADEMARK STATUS; DECORATORS MUST SORT THROUGH THE OFFERINGS IN A MARKETPLACE SUCH AS THIS TO BE SURE THEY GO HOME WITH THE SURPRISE AND NOT THE CLICHÉ.

✳ ✳ ✳

Below, top to bottom: SOMETIMES YOU CAN'T SEE THE FOREST FOR THE MOOSE; MORE SIGNS OF THE TIMES; ANGLING ART IS WHERE YOU FIND IT.

emptied out their barns and attics for the day. All are animated by an unmistakable *joie de vendre,* and both serious collectors and browsers brake for their rustic crafts.

"It has become a community event," says Oliver. "The two churches in town hold church suppers over the weekend, and the firehouse does a barbecue. The Friday preview party, an important fund-raiser for the museum, now draws three hundred or more. And people come to this show ready to buy. In one recent year, a dealer came up with two trucks full of materials and sold out in twenty minutes after the show opened on Saturday morning. Another dealer was talking to so many customers he lost his voice by noon."

Some show-goers stay over to immerse themselves in the collections of the museum proper. In addition to unmatched holdings of Adirondack art and furnishings, there are permanent exhibitions on the role of boats and boating in these mountains; the age of horses, with fifty horse-drawn vehicles for work and recreation on display; and detailed glimpses into the life of a logging camp and a mining town of the era, logging and mining being the two principal industries in the early economy of the region. For students of the Adirondack house style, the museum compound has an original log hotel, built in 1876, the cottage and studio of landscape painter Gustave Wiegand, a log hunting camp, the wildnerness cabin of dime-store adventure novelist Ned Buntline, and a one-room schoolhouse built in 1907. For something completely different, there is the not-of-Microsoft-fame Bill Gates Diner, a former trolley operated as a popular eatery by one Bill and Dawn Gates in Bolton Landing, New York, from 1949 to 1980.

Jerry Oliver believes that Adirondack rustic art and furnishings are in a stage of rediscovery at this time that resembles the frenzy over folk art in the 1960s. Part of the reason was the spurt in second-home construction due to the booming economy. "People are building these luxury log homes in the country," he says, noting in passing that the show is pulling heavily from Colorado and Georgia, "and they are looking for one-of-a-kind pieces to decorate them with. The best things fly off the field."

The stuffed moose did not fly, but there's always next year.

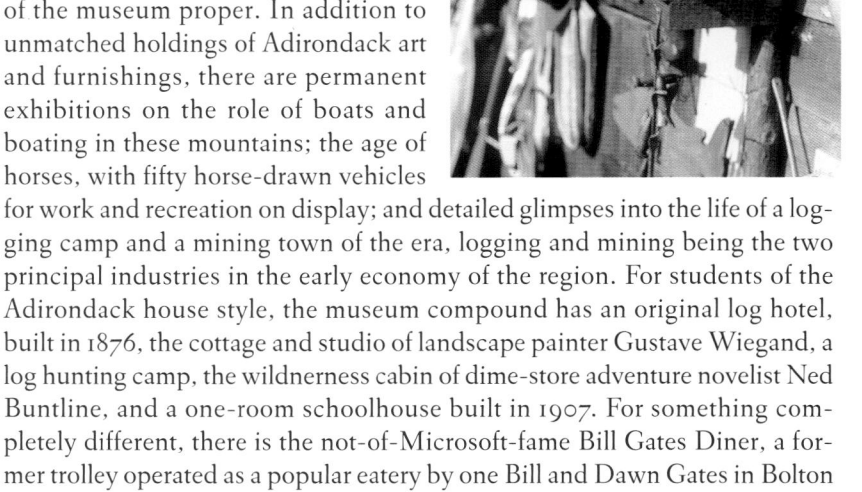

Above left: A HARDY BROTHERS FLY WALLET FROM ENGLAND, MADE IN THE 1920S AND BURSTING WITH FLIES, WAS OFFERED FOR $1,285 BY MALE ANTIQUE DECOR OF ROXBURY, CONNECTICUT.

* * *

Below left: AFTER AN EXHAUSTING BUT SUCCESSFUL DAY OF SHOPPING FOR SPORTING ITEMS, STEVE BREUNING OF ROCHESTER HILLS, MICHIGAN, TOOK A WELCOME BREAK.

* * *

Below: COLORFUL BOBBERS AND LURES WERE AT EVERY TURN, WAITING TO GET THEIR HOOKS INTO A BUYER.

* * *

Overleaf: A STATELY EVOCATION OF THE RUSTIC LOOK FROM BERT AND NANCY SAVAGE OF LARCH LODGE, CENTER STRAFFORD, NEW HAMPSHIRE.

3
COASTAL
WATERS

"NO WAY THIS IS fishing, Doc. This is hunting," says Albert Ponzoa, as he poles his skiff through the mouthwash-blue flats of Marathon in the Florida Keys. From his raised platform in the stern of the boat, he is scanning the water for stingrays coming into the flats to feed on crabs as the full moon tide advances. Cobias and bonefish often will jump on top of the marauding rays to feed off the bits of food kicked up in their wake. "That's a lemon shark off the top of my pole," he notes, adding laconically, "Sharks are harmless 'til they bite you."

Ponzoa's client, standing at the bow of the boat with fly rod in hand, laughs appreciatively. He has had a good morning, the climax being his tying into a 37-inch bonefish with a Clouser minnow fly. His name is Carl, but Albert calls everyone Doc, Doctor, or Bubba. A former teacher and the son of Cuban immigrants,

> **THERE ARE**
>
> ....
>
> **FISH THAT WILL**
>
> ....
>
> **NEVER DIE AT**
>
> ....
>
> **THE HANDS**
>
> ....
>
> **OF MAN.**
>
> ....
>
> —*Linda Greenlaw*

Ponzoa is one of approximately 550 Coast Guard–certified fishing captains in the Keys, with so many referrals he is out fishing—hunting—with anglers hundreds of days a year. Keys guides have a reputation for being demanding, and some customers don't like the idea of shelling out $300 to $400 a day just to be shouted at for shanking a cast. Ponzoa seldom guides rank beginners, but his knowledge, enthusiasm, and repartee make him good company, even if he is candid about faulty execution. "Bones at three o'clock at ten feet!" he had cried at an earlier location, then groaned, "Oh, Jesus, I'm dying up here, Doctor," after Carl slapped his line on the water at one o'clock and spooked the fish.

But Carl makes amends in the afternoon. On a bank near a place called Alligator Light, Albert sees mud and sickle tails: "Lookit all the permit coming at you at

11:30, yahoo!" Carl makes a decent crosswind cast and his fly, a Merkin crab, lands with a pop in their midst and provokes an instantaneous reaction. "Did he want to eat that fly or what!" cries Albert as the permit runs in the direction of a mangrove island in the distance. "That sucker was ravenous! Look, he's smokin'! Strip line! Strip line!" It takes twenty minutes to tire the fish and bring it to the boat. Shaped like a pompano and blazingly iridescent, the permit measures 36 inches. There's time for Albert to snap Carl with the fish with Carl's camera, then it's released unharmed. Both guide and angler are jubilant. Says Albert, "This is what it's all about!"

Of course, not all expeditions into the brine end on such a positive note. On another day, up in mainland Florida, five guys, jackdaw raw beginners in the sport of angling, peel off from a business meeting and hire a local guide with a sporty runabout to take them fishing in coastal waters for half a day. It is so choppy the guide himself gets seasick; he vomits in the guise of checking one of the trolling lines. His clients spend most of the morning fumbling the live shrimp and pintail baits, untangling their casts, and removing hooks

from their thumbs and shirts, meanwhile inhaling a steady diet of diesel fumes—and a couple of Buds. When they finally land a few small snappers, the Stooges (as they have billed themselves) decide to chop up the catch to use for bait, in the hope of landing larger fish, but this operation leaves the deck slimy with oil and blood. Finally, one of their number does tie into a large barracuda, but his rod, a cheap rental, snaps in two. A fellow Stooge helps him land the thing, however. The 'cuda thrashes about at their feet, its pointy teeth flashing in the harsh winter light. Fighting queasy stomachs and feeling mortally threatened by this creature of the deep, the guys dance across the deck as the boat dips with the waves, slipping and sliding, hollering and spluttering, cracking shins and elbows against hard surfaces and each other in their maniacal spin-the-bottle avoidance of *Jaws III.* Eventually someone manages to cut the line, another grabs the fish by the tail and unloads it overboard, and all breathe a sigh of relief. The guide turns his boat around and they head for home, sported out.

Fishing in freshwater lakes and streams, anglers have a pretty good idea of what they are likely to catch, or not

Above: NORTH OF FORT MYERS ON THE GULF SIDE OF FLORIDA, THE BOCA GRANDE LIGHTHOUSE HAS STOOD AT THE SOUTHERN TIP OF GASPARILLA ISLAND SINCE 1890. HERE, IN THE FERTILE CONFLUENCE OF CHARLOTTE HARBOR, PINE ISLAND SOUND, AND THE GULF, WATERS TEEM WITH GAME AND FOOD FISH, INCLUDING FLOUNDER, POMPANO, SNOOK, GROUPER, REDFISH, MANGROVE SNAPPER, KINGFISH, MACKEREL, AND, IN THE SPRING AND SUMMER, MIGRATING TARPON.

catch, on any given day, because the fish population in those relatively shallow and confined bodies of water is known and finite and by and large not very menacing. Fishing in the ocean, however, even near shore, anglers are never quite sure of what lurks below a surface that is never still. Surf casting for bluefish on the Outer Banks of North Carolina, a woman of a certain age hooked into a huge stingray. "After it leaped out of the water once," her husband relates, "she merely gave the rod to me and told me it was my problem. I wasn't able to stop it as it raced back toward the open sea."

Even when fishing from bridges and piers over salt water, anglers are exposed to a veritable Noah's Ark of ocean life. Lined up along the legendary 1,140-foot Pacifica Pier in San Francisco Bay, they catch salmon, smelt, Pacific cod, leopard shark, and 57 (almost) varieties of a saltwater panfish called surfperch. The main trick in pier fishing, if the angler doesn't have a drop net, is keeping what is caught on the hook while reeling it up through the naked air for 20 or 30 feet. If in a day on the Pacifica you catch one each of the barred surfperch native to southern California, the calico surfperch of central California, and the redtail surfperch of northern waters, you will have scored the exalted trifecta of pier-

fishing in San Francisco, according to California pier-fishing expert Ken Jones.

Deep-sea fishing elicits the most awe and, at times, terror, in that by definition it brings the angler in close proximity to the largest and most dangerous pelagic creatures of all. Melville writes, near the calamitous end of *Moby Dick*: "Hither, and thither, on high, glided the snow-white wings of small, unspeckled birds; these were the gentle thoughts of the feminine air, but to and fro in the deeps, far down in the bottomless blue, rushed mighty leviathans, swordfish, and sharks; and these were the strong, troubled murderous thinkings of the masculine sea."

Even an experienced commercial boat captain like Linda Greenlaw was taken aback by the murderous thinkings of a swordfish that she and her crew members tried unsuccessfully to land aboard her *Hannah Boden* out of Gloucester, Massachusetts, a century and a half after Ahab's ship left Nantucket. After the swordfish broke off its line and sank from sight, following a long, arduous struggle, she reported in her book, *The Hungry Ocean*: "The five men who called me Captain were all that kept me from crying tears of frustration. Nobody uttered a sound. Suddenly, and unexpectedly, the giant

Above: THE CANAL ALONG THE TAMIAMI TRAIL, RUNNING THROUGH THE HEART OF THE EVERGLADES, INVITES FISHING FROM ITS BANKS AND FROM BOATS, PROVIDED ANGLERS REMAIN MINDFUL OF THE EVER-PRESENT ALLIGATORS. *Overleaf:* A PAIR OF FISHY ROADSIDE ATTRACTIONS ON PINE ISLAND, ONE OF THE BARRIER ISLANDS ALONG THE COAST IN SOUTHWEST FLORIDA.

fish shot out from under the boat and swam through the water into which we all stared. The fish swam on its side, glaring up at us with one big eye, and stayed near the surface until it was out of sight again, its victory lap completed."

Pleasanter surprises await the fisherman nearer to shore, in the coastal waters where most sportfishing is conducted, and yet this saltwater habitat is also a combination of risk and reward. For millennial anglers, casting with a fly rod has replaced heaving line from beach or jetty with a heavy surf-casting rod, or trolling from a boat with spinning tackle or buckets of bait. The current rise in popularity of saltwater fly-fishing, which *Sports Afield* writer Jack Samson calls "freshwater fishing on steroids," began in the Florida Keys with the development of light-tackle techniques in the years immediately following World War II by guides like Jimmie Albright, George Hommel, Joe Brooks, and Lefty Kreh, and other sportsmen like Boston Red Sox great Ted Williams, who moved his winter home to Islamorada, in the Keys, just to be near the action. The pioneers discovered that hunting powerful game fish with lightweight gear and artificial flies was a testing but exhilarating departure from earlier, clumsier methods.

In more recent years the same tools and techniques—and even in some cases the same flats boats—have been adapted for pursuing striped bass, bluefish, and false albacore in the shallows along the eastern seaboard, big redfish and schools of sea trout in the marshes off the Carolinas and in the Gulf of Mexico, off the coast of Louisiana and Texas, barracuda and bonito in the shallows around San Diego, and record stripers in Oregon's Coos Bay, to name just a few of the fresh new targets for the fly rod. Manufac-

turers of rods, reels, and lines have caught saltwater fever, flooding the market with new and better designs of fly-fishing gear.

"The minimal amount of equipage needed for fly-fishing appeals to me," wrote Nelson Bryant, longtime outdoor writer for the *New York Times,* in a newspaper column explaining why he had become deeply hooked by the sport: "Gone are the lures, tackle boxes, sand spikes and messy bait or bait buckets. I can stroll along miles of beach with a few dozen flies tucked in one pocket, prospecting all the likely water with a rod that weighs only a few ounces."

Not everyone buys into the mystique of saltwater fly-fishing, however. "The snobbery of fly fishermen really irks me, especially the dilettantes with their never-ending odes to the spirituality of casting a fly to such species as bonefish, tarpon, and permit," says John F. Reiger, an ardent sportsman and history professor at Ohio University, who grew up fishing with spinning tackle in the 1950s under the tutelage of Tommy Gifford, a well-respected guide of that era. "I continue to use what I have always used for traditional reasons," Reiger declares, "including conventional open-faced saltwater outfits, and I'll put many of my long battles up against the fly fisherman anytime—like a $11\frac{1}{2}$-pound bonefish on 8-pound spinning tackle, caught among a myriad of mangrove islets; or a 117-pound, 6-foot 4-inch tarpon caught with 30-pound test conventional gear, *but* from an anchored boat in shallow water, with the motor down, and with no fighting chair or rod belt."

But whatever the equipment in the angler's hand, there is no gainsaying the thrill of an alien force announcing itself at the other end of one's line, and the satisfaction of reeling it in.

Above: WHETHER THE FISHING IS FOR BIG GAME IN THE PACIFIC, OR STALKING STRIPED BASS IN THE MARSHES OF CHESAPEAKE BAY, AMERICA'S COASTAL WATERS BECKON ANGLERS THROUGHOUT THE YEAR.
Opposite: IN THE BONEFISH FLATS OFF MARATHON, FLORIDA, KEYS FISHING GUIDE ALBERT PONZOA HAS BROUGHT CLIENT TOM SADLER WITHIN CASTING DISTANCE OF ONE OF THE BULLETS OF THE FLATS.

OLD SALTS IN A NEW WORLD

CALIFORNIA SALTWATER FISHING TRADITIONS

A HUNDRED YEARS AGO, yellowtail tuna were so abundant off the coast of southern California's Catalina Island that fishermen would throw heavy hand lines into their midst from the shore and drag up onto the beach whatever they managed to snag-hook. Then they would butcher the fish, leaving the carcasses for sharks.

This practice appalled a naturalist and author of that era by the name of Charles Frederick Holder, a recent transplant from Massachusetts, where he had been schooled in the art of fishing with light freshwater tackle. Dr. Holder decided to organize a fishing club that would uphold a more sportsmanlike approach to angling, one in which the fish was more nearly an equal partner of the fisherman in the sport and there was less bloody mayhem present around the edges. In 1898, along with seven other like-minded fellows, he founded the Tuna Club on the front porch of one of the hotels on the island, with exactly that approach as the guiding principle for landing tuna, broadbill swordfish, and marlin. "Under the rules and with the tackle of that time," says club historian Mike Farrior, "the fish was as liable to get away as he was to be caught after he was hooked."

To this day, the Tuna Club officially recognizes only catches made

with a single hook, and on nonstretch linen and Dacron rather than the more easily fished monofilament line. Light tackle records are limited to 6- or 9-thread line (20- to 30-pound test), and the heavy tackle line is limited to 24-thread. During the actual catch, only the fisherman may handle the rod, and only one other person mans the gaff.

In the very first summer

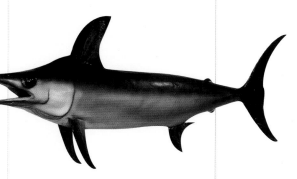

Above: A CATCH OF PRODIGIOUS SIZE BY AN EARLY MEMBER, THIS 573-POUND SWORDFISH OCCUPIES A PLACE OF HONOR IN THE CLUB'S TROPHY ROOM.

* * *

Left: ALTHOUGH MEMBERSHIP IN THE TUNA CLUB IS BY INVITATION ONLY, ANGLERS CAN FISH THE SAME WATERS; MOST FISHING CHARTERS ARE ARRANGED AT LANDINGS IN THE MAINLAND CITIES OF LONG BEACH OR

Right: THE TOWN OF AVALON, RISING INTO THE HILLS ABOVE THE TUNA CLUB, IS A POPULAR WEEKEND DESTINATION FOR MAINLANDERS, WITH GREAT SHOPS, RELAXED RESTAURANTS, AND OTHER PLACES OF INTEREST. ZANE GREY PUEBLO HOTEL ON THE ISLAND IS THE FORMER HOME OF THE FAMOUS WESTERN AUTHOR AND ANGLER. THE INN ON MOUNT ADA, WITH ITS SPECTACULAR VIEW OF THE BAY, IS THE FORMER HOME OF CHEWING GUM MOGUL WILLIAM WRIGLEY JR.

Above: THE TUNA CLUB WAS A MECCA FOR CELEBRITY ANGLERS IN THE EARLY DECADES OF THE 20TH CENTURY, AND MEMENTOS OF THEIR VISITS CAN BE FOUND ON THE WALLS AND IN THE TROPHY CASES OF THE CLUB MEETING ROOM. AMONG THOSE WHO FISHED OUT OF THE TUNA CLUB WERE WINSTON CHURCHILL, CHARLIE CHAPLIN, ZANE GREY, CECIL B. DEMILLE, AND GENERAL GEORGE S. PATTON.

of the club's existence, Dr. Holder showed that he practiced what he preached, landing a 183-pound bluefin tuna with a relatively flimsy rod and reel. In fact, he and his boatman were pulled 10 miles during the four-hour battle to reel the fish in. The feat put the club and its founder in headlines around the world.

The club's storied history is captured in the old portraits and early artifacts of saltwater sportfishing that blanket the walls of its clubhouse overlooking Avalon Bay. The gaff and its beautifully carved box on display were presented to the club by Winston Churchill after he went fishing with club member Ben Meyer in 1929.

"Churchill had always wanted to fish here," relates Farrior. "He jumped ship from the British fleet on maneuvers off Catalina at the time, got on Meyer's launch, and promptly caught a marlin just outside the bay. Mind you, some members had fished these waters for years and had never caught a marlin. Afterward, Churchill came into the Bait Box [the club's tiny bar], mixed himself a gin and tonic and declared, 'I say, that was grand fun. I see why you chaps enjoy this club so much.'"

Other famous people who fished here and lived to tell about it in the Bait Box included General George S. Patton, Charlie Chaplin, Stan Laurel, Jackie Coogan, and Cecil B. DeMille. Zane Grey was a club member from 1913 to 1923, when he was forced to resign, according to one report, after questioning whether the club president's wife had actually caught a 426-pound swordfish unassisted.

To this day, the Tuna Club has maintained its rigorous standards. Membership is by invitation only and requires candidates to have in some way helped protect and advance big-game fishing. "To give the fish a fair chance for its life was, and is, the intent of the club," says Farrior.

COTTAGE BY THE BAY

ARTIST'S OUTPOST ON MARYLAND'S EASTERN SHORE

WHEN HE WAS A KID, C. D. Clarke was so possessed by fishing that he thought nothing of riding his bike for two hours to get to a good trout stream. He collected caddis and mayfly nymphs off the bottom of one local stream with his makeshift nylon-stocking net, then kept them alive in an aquarium tank, complete with oxygenating bubbler, until they metamorphosed into a host of flying insects in the room.

"I'd have a Hendrickson hatch in my own bedroom," Clarke relates.

Even today, as a sporting artist, C. D. Clarke pursues his chosen career in a way that seems as much sport as it is art. A recent commission from an outfitter in Iceland allowed him to spend a week fishing for salmon and Arctic char in that country's rivers, producing nine paintings along the way. Clarke's work captures the feeling of the myriad places he has visited, from sparkling bonefish flats and misty Scottish salmon rivers to the icy mountain reaches of the Chilean Andes and the warm sunny pampas of Argentina.

The paintings seem to "convey emotion in landscape," as one critic has observed, an achievement hard-won by the artist through years of observation and practice. "All my knowledge of light and how things would be recorded and responded to in the outdoors came from my early years of working outdoors on location," Clarke says. "What you learn about light and color in the field is indispensable."

Born in Rochester, New York, C. D. Clarke took his interest in the outdoors to Syracuse University, enrolling in a program

Opposite: C. D. CLARKE'S OIL PAINTING *DREDGING THE BRIDGE* SHOWS AN ANGLER BLIND-FISHING TO STRUCTURE WITH A SINKING LINE ON A CHANNEL UNDER INDIAN KEY BRIDGE IN THE FLORIDA KEYS. THE FRAMED PHOTO BELOW THE PICTURE IS OF THE ARTIST'S MOTHER, ALISON CLARKE, OF ROCHESTER, NEW YORK.

Above: ALTHOUGH THE HOUSE IS ABOUT A HUNDRED YEARS OLD, ITS EXACT AGE IS UNKNOWN. A REAL ESTATE FRIEND TOLD THEM IT WOULD SEEM MORE VALUABLE IF IT HAD BEEN BUILT BEFORE THE TURN OF THE CENTURY, SO THE CLARKES HAD THIS SIGN MADE AS A JOKE.

* * *

Left: THE CARVED WOOD ATLANTIC SALMON WITH INSCRIPTION WAS MADE BY A FRIEND OF CHRIS CLARKE, VIRGINIA ARTIST MORTEN FADUM.

Above: IN THE ARTIST'S STUDIO, LANDSCAPES EXECUTED ON SITE AT SEVERAL ANGLING VENUES AWAIT FINISHING DETAILS; THOSE IN THE TOP ROW DOCUMENT A TROUT FISHING EXPEDITION ON THE RIO SIMSON AND RIO MANUELES IN CHILE.

* * *

Below: EVERY MAY, ALMOST EVERY YEAR, CLARKE TOWS HIS FLATS SKIFF TO FLORIDA FOR A MONTH OF TARPON FISHING.

that ultimately would have led to forestry school, "but after one semester," he says, "I realized that forestry was chemistry and math, so I turned to art. I did nothing for three years but paint. It didn't matter how the paintings turned out, I just did them. That's when I learned to enjoy everything I could about landscape and about the process of watercolor."

Chris met his future wife, Iris, also an art major, in college, and after graduation they married and moved to Maryland's Eastern Shore. Chesapeake Bay, which separates that shore from the rest of the state, covers 2,500 square miles, a huge estuary system where the fresh water of inland rivers mingles with the salt water of the ocean, and the Clarke house is smack in the middle of this aquatic life, in the island town of Frenchtown. "The real estate agent showed us this house on the island surrounded by the salt marshes," he recalls. The entire settlement of Frenchtown still counts fewer than twenty dwellings. "The vastness and openness of the location made it feel as if we were on some Serengeti Plain. But the place itself was a wreck. You could see the sun through the roof and there was a dead bird in the toilet bowl. We asked [the agent] if the owners would rent it and he said, 'Hell, it's so cheap you might as well buy it.'"

And that's what they did, fixing the place up as they went. Like their house, the surrounding marshes are attempting a comeback after a century of neglect. The Chesapeake is the natural habitat for some 250 types of fish, crabs, clams, and oysters, although overharvesting, combined with pollutants from industry and sediments from farms, has decimated many species. Shad and yellow perch, once present in huge numbers, are struggling to rebound under newly introduced conservation policies. Migrating waterfowl, which once blackened Chesapeake skies and waters every winter, have also been in decline.

"But things have improved since we've been here," Clarke believes, "especially in our immediate area. There are places where I can fish today that were devoid of aquatic grasses seventeen years ago."

Left: IN THE FRONT HALLWAY, TIM BORSKI'S PORTRAIT OF AN ATLANTIC SALMON RECORDS THE 27-POUNDER CAUGHT BY C. D. CLARKE ON THE TWEED RIVER IN SCOTLAND IN 1984, THE LARGEST FISH OF THE SEASON FOR THAT BEAT. OBSCURED BY THE DOOR IS A PAINTING OF GUNNER, A CHESAPEAKE BAY RETRIEVER ONCE OWNED BY THE CLARKES.

* * *

Below: IRIS CLARKE FLY-FISHES FOR STRIPERS FROM THE FLATS SKIFF, AMONG HAMMOCKS NOT MUCH MORE THAN A MILE FROM HER FRONT DOOR.

Opposite: AMID THE JUMBLE OF
PAINTS AND BRUSHES IN THE
STUDIO IS A NEARLY FINISHED
PAINTING OF A QUAIL SHOOTING
PARTY ON THE FAMOUS KING
RANCH IN TEXAS.

* * *

Left: WINDRUSH COTTAGE, AS
SEEN FROM THE CRAB HOUSE
ACROSS THE WAY.

* * *

Below: THE STRIPER FLY IN THE
VISE WAS TIED BY TIM BORSKI, A
FRIEND OF THE CLARKES WHO
LIVES IN ISLAMORADA, FLORIDA,
WHERE HE PAINTS UNDERWATER
FISH SCENES AND ALSO CREATES
BEST-SELLING SALTWATER FLY
PATTERNS FOR UMPQUA FEATHER
MERCHANTS ON THE UMPQUA
RIVER IN OREGON.

ISLAND LOST IN TIME

CABBAGE KEY, PRECIOUS REMNANT OF OLD FLORIDA

"C ABBAGE KEY ISN'T an island, it's a state of mind," says Rob Wells, who bought this rare surviving piece of very old Florida, hard by the Gulf Coast Intracoastal Waterway near Fort Myers, in 1976. A previous owner, Florida artist Larry Stultz, had turned the private residence on the island into a getaway catering to wealthy tarpon, snook, and redfish fishermen and other artists and writers, including John D. MacDonald.

Stultz's self-portrait is still found over the fireplace in the bar, which itself is a state of mind, its walls papered with about $28,000 in autographed dollar bills. "The story goes that an angler tacked the first bill up to be sure he had a dollar to buy a beer the next time he stopped in," explains Wells, who has taken pains not to change anything about the inn, restaurant, and sprinkling of cottages on the 100-acre key, "because those who come back want the place as they remember it." It's rumored that singer Jimmy Buffett, who has visited several times by waterplane, wrote his song "Cheeseburger in Paradise" as a paean to the island's offbeat charm.

Some visitors never leave Cabbage Key. Terry Forgie stopped here for a night on his way to Jamaica by boat twenty or so years ago and has been here ever since, working as the dockmaster. "Cabbage Key has a spirituality about it you don't find anyplace else," he says. "People sense it. They consider it their discovery, their private little paradise."

Archaeologists believe the key may have been occupied on and off for more than 5,000 years. At 38 feet above sea level, it's one of the highest points

Opposite: A VINTAGE PHOTOGRAPH FROM THE 1950S WAS USED TO KICK OFF A SNOOK FISHING TOURNAMENT THAT HAS BECOME AN ANNUAL SPRING FIXTURE ON THE CALENDAR AT CABBAGE KEY. THE CHARITY FUND-RAISER IS NAMED FOR FLOYD "FINGERS" O'BANNON, A LEGENDARY LOCAL GUIDE WHO, IN AN ERA BEFORE LIMITS WERE PLACED ON COMMERCIAL SNOOK FISHING, CONSIDERED IT A POOR DAY IF HE DIDN'T COME BACK FROM FISHING WITH AT LEAST 1,000 POUNDS OF SNOOK FILLETS.

* * *

Above: LOCATED AT MARKER 60 ON THE GULF INTERCOASTAL WATERWAY IN PINE ISLAND SOUND, CABBAGE KEY IS A POPULAR LUNCH DESTINATION FOR SAILORS, ANGLERS, AND TOURISTS PASSING THROUGH THE AREA.

* * *

Left: WILDLIFE IS IN ABUNDANCE ON AND AROUND THE LUSH, UNCONVENTIONAL 100-ACRE ISLAND, WHERE A DOG ONCE SERVED AS THE UNOFFICIAL MAYOR.

in this part of Florida: early Calusa Indians used it to dump shells and over the years the refuse piled up into a mound, or midden.

The locale's modern angling traditions began in 1929 when Alan and Grace Houghton Rinehart bought the entire key for $2,500 and built a winter retreat atop the mound. "The Rineharts came here because of the tarpon fishing," says Wells. "They were avid fishermen."

Alan's mother, Mary Roberts Rinehart, a popular mystery writer of the 1920s and 1930s, was present during early construction of the main house and influenced some of the architectural and engineering innovations, including a solar energy system, six working fireplaces, five porches, a storm shelter, and a rainwater-collection system with a capacity of 25,000 gallons.

A nature lover, Mrs. Rinehart was perhaps inspired by the trails winding around the island among cabbage palms, royal poincianas, wild orchids, and live oaks draped with air plants and Spanish moss. There is no evidence, however, that she wrote any of her fifty-eight novels while staying here.

Every spring, Cabbage Key hosts the Fingers O'Bannon Snook Tournament, named after a legendary guide, which has raised more than $150,000 for the marine sciences department of Florida Gulf Coast University. Snook have been described as "nuclear-powered bass" and are found feeding in the surf in June and July and touring backcountry mangroves of Pine Island Sound to the lower Everglades over the winter. The snook-fishing fund-raiser is in keeping with a tradition of wildlife conservation on the island. Tarpon Cottage, one of six cottages where visitors can stay, if not in a room in the inn, was a tarpon research lab in the 1930s, founded and funded by the Rinehart family.

Beginning in May, tarpon fishing in local waters is also extraordinary, while some hunt the "Silver King" pods from local beaches, many fish the Boca Grande pass where the fish congregate, says Rob Wells. "Some days more than 10,000 fish fill the pass, with many jumping and rolling continuously. At times you could almost walk across the pass on the backs of tarpon!"

Above: ARTIST LARRY STULTZ, WHOSE SELF-PORTRAIT HANGS IN THE BAR, BOUGHT CABBAGE KEY IN 1944 AND TURNED IT INTO A MODEST INN CATERING TO TARPON FISHERMAN, MANY OF WHOM FOLLOWED THE TRADITION OF THE PATRON WHO PINNED AN AUTOGRAPHED DOLLAR TO THE WALL IN CASE HE CAME BACK ONE DAY WITHOUT SUFFICIENT FUNDS FOR A BEER AND A SANDWICH.

* * *

Opposite: THE SIGN AT CABBAGE KEY WELCOMES VISITORS WITH A PLEA FOR WATER CONSERVATION: "SHOWER WITH A FRIEND."

YES — The shrimp are small.
NO — I don't know why.
YES — They are all the same.
NO — I can't pick you all big ones.
YES — I know you're a good customer.
NO — You can't pick them yourself.
YES — There is still 12 in a dozen.
NO — We don't have live mullet. (UNTIL MARCH 1)
YES — I lose count if I answer questions.
NO — I don't grow them, just buy and sell.
YES — They are always small in summer.

**Any Further Questions
Ask The Shrimp**

HOOK, LINE, AND SINKER

FISHING EMPORIUM ON THE OVERSEAS HIGHWAY

NOT LONG AFTER "Captain Dave" Brown took over the business in 1991, an elderly local angler came into the Tackle Box, a Marathon, Florida, institution of some vintage itself, having opened in 1943 when the population in town numbered fewer than a thousand and lighting still came from kerosene lamps.

"The man wanted me to fix this fishing rod he brought in that he'd been using for thirty years or more," Brown recalls. "It was an amazing piece of work, with four or five different guides on it and a patched-together handle. It was such an authentic relic of fishing in the Florida Keys that I traded him a brand-new rod for it on the spot—he couldn't believe my offer! Anyway, I hung his old rod over the door inside the shop with a $10,000 sales tag— you know, like a lucky horseshoe."

And so far luck has been with the Fort Lauderdale–raised entrepreneur who moved to South Carolina in 1971 to work in construction there for twenty years. "Then I retired, moved back to Florida, and bought the Tackle Box," he relates with a chuckle, "and now I'm having fun sixty hours a week."

Tens of millions of dollars' worth of exotic-looking merchandise flow through America's bait-and-tackle shops every year, from Calcutta ballyhoo (bait) to single hook monofilament rigs (tackle) to titanium waders, but Brown's store has a timeless air that sets it apart from most. "Customers told me, 'Don't change a thing, we like the relaxed atmosphere,'" he says, "so we've kept the place pretty much as we found it." It also has a sleepy golden retriever named Chelsea, because, says Dave, "you can't have a tackle shop without a dog."

Unlike some tackle shops, Brown's shop is in business to help folks catch fish, and he and his staff offer not just "the best-looking and

Opposite: AS THE SIGN INDICATES, YOU'RE PRETTY MUCH ON YOUR OWN IN THE BACK ROOM OF THE TACKLE BOX AT MILE MARKER 48 IN THE FLORIDA KEYS.

* * *

Left: IN A BUILDING DATING FROM 1943, THE TACKLE SHOP IN MARATHON IS ONE OF THE OLDEST IN THE MIDDLE KEYS.

* * *

Below: FITTINGLY, A TOP-OF-THE-FOOD-CHAIN HAMMERHEAD SHARK OCCUPIES THE TOP OF THE SIGN THAT THE TACKLE BOX RELIES UPON TO LURE IMPULSE SHOPPERS OFF THE OVERSEAS HIGHWAY. A HAMMERHEAD THREE TIMES ITS SIZE, KNOWN AS BIG MO, APPEARS NEAR THE BAHIA HONDA BRIDGE IN MARATHON DURING THE SPRING TARPON RUN EVERY YEAR, WAITS FOR A TARPON IN THE 100-POUND RANGE TO SWIM BY, AND DEVOURS IT IN ONE BITE.

luckiest hats anywhere"—fishermen are superstitious about their hats —but a skilled fishing reel repair and reconditioning program, backed up by 20,000 parts in stock and such homegrown tools as Dave's Dolphin Demon, better known as the "Triple D." It's a rigged bait that simulates a flying fish during reentry, complete with bubbles. And there is a state-of-the-art electronic system spilling out hourly forecasts about where the fish called dolphin are biting. As in retailing, "in fishing the Keys," says Captain Dave, "location is everything."

When he's not in the shop or winning fishing tournaments such as the Key West Classic, Brown takes charters on his 30-foot twin diesel Topaz in quest of permit, cobia, snappers, groupers, and giant jewfish, the largest member of the grouper family. Clients fish from the coral reef to the edge of what Brown calls "the mightiest river in the world"—the Gulf Stream. The very best fishing appears to be had over the many hapless wrecks at the bottom of the Gulf of Mexico about 35 to 40 miles from Marathon, most of them ships that were used as targets for bombing practice by the U.S. Navy during World War II.

All year long, the back room at the Tackle Box, where the bait tanks are kept, is literally aswim with live shrimp, pinfish, and crabs. But the basic bait-and-tackle attitude is at play here as it is in the rest of the shop, exemplified by a sign over one of the tanks:

Yes—the shrimp are small.
No—I don't know why.
Any Further Questions,
Ask the Shrimp.

Below: WITH REELS AND REELS OF COLORFUL TRILENE FISHING LINE STACKED UNDER THE WORKBENCH, KEITH SULLIVAN WORKS ON AN INTRICATE FLY REEL REPAIR FOR A CUSTOMER. WITH 20,000 PARTS IN STOCK, OWNER DAVE BROWN DOES A LAND-OFFICE BUSINESS IN ROD AND REEL REPAIRS. "WE'VE GOT EVERYTHING TO CATCH THE FISH," SAYS CAPTAIN BROWN, "EXCEPT GAS FOR THE BOAT."

Left and above: BASKETS OF
ASSORTED TROLLING SKIRTS
HANG FROM THE SHOP CEILING.
THE SKIRTS ARE USED TO DRESS
NATURAL BAITS LIKE BALLYHOO
WITH THEIR FISH-ATTRACTING
COLORS. CAPTAIN BROWN, WHO
STARTED FISHING IN 1957, SAYS
THAT FISHING IN THE KEYS
IMPROVED IN THE 1990S WITH
THE INTRODUCTION OF REGULA-
TIONS BANNING FISH TRAPS, SOME
AS LARGE AS ROOM-SIZED, AND
ENTANGLING GILL NETS, SOME AS
LARGE AS A QUARTER MILE WIDE.
REDFISH, SEA TROUT, SPANISH
MACKERAL, AND SNOOK WERE
AMONG THE SPECIES DECIMATED
BY COMMERCIAL NETTING
PRACTICES, BUT THOSE SPECIES,
ALONG WITH MOST BAIT FISH,
HAVE SINCE MADE A COMEBACK.

ENDLESS SUMMER

FISHING PARADISE OF THE "CONCH REPUBLIC"

IT WAS NOT UNTIL March of 1938 that a traveler could drive a car all 200 miles from Key Largo to Key West without puddle-hopping by ferry along the way. With the completion of the two-lane Overseas Highway in that year, it became possible to traverse this extraordinary archipelago of islands and reefs entirely by car, and it is still the best way to take the full measure of North America's most exotic destination.

Key Largo, the film noir classic with Humphrey Bogart and Edward G. Robinson, captures the end-of-the-road, end-of-the-world fatalism that a trip to the Keys can inspire. After a caper, the gangsters hole up in a house in Key Largo, but a hurricane blows in and all hell breaks loose. Never mind that the film was shot on a soundstage in California, it nicely conveys the romantic-outlaw culture that many longtime Keys residents embrace to this day. In the real Key Largo, by the way, is found the boat navigated by Bogart in another landmark film not shot in the Keys: *The African Queen*. It's tied to a dock at the Holiday Inn.

Incongruity is a signature of life in the Keys. Seedy trailer parks butt up to luxury resorts. Ring-nosed babes on million-dollar yachts drop anchor next to ramshackle floating churches. Funky bait shops adjoin gourmet eateries. One minute it's the Gold Coast, the next, the Redneck Riviera. In Key West, the good, the bad, and the ugly exist in about the same amounts, only here it's all magnified theatrically, perhaps because this town is the do-not-pass-go final stop in the game; only 90 miles separate it from the next landmass, Cuba. Some visitors find the Ernest Hemingway house, sparsely furnished and crawling with mutant cats, depressing, and bars trading on the legend of Papa the Drinker seem to attract their fair share of louts and cruise ship refugees. But dozens of famous nonalcoholic writers have lived in this town, too, and bookstores are almost as common as drinking spots.

Key West's most charming feature is a hundred-block historic district of wooden

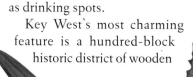

houses in a host of Caribbean-inspired architectural styles. In Old Town's cemetery, tombs are aboveground, New Orleans style, and one sports a much-quoted epitaph: "I told you I was sick." Duvall Street, the main drag, is a mixture of chic and cheap, but if you walk it without pause, you'll get from the Atlantic Ocean to the Gulf of Mexico in less than half an hour. If nothing else, it shows how vulnerable the slender string of islands is to hurricanes. But people are the real attraction in Key West, whether they're twenty thousand bikers showing off their Harleys and tattoos, or an equal number of exhibitionists—gay, straight, and indeterminate—in costume for the annual Halloween celebration, called Fantasy Fest. What might Harry S. Truman, the Missouri-born president who fished and played cards with his cronies in the Keys back in the 1940s, have made of it all?

Fishing is the central organizing principle of this place of turquoise waters and hallucinogenic skies. No other area in the contiguous states offers more fish to fish for (more than a thousand species), more ways to fish for them, and more year-round opportunities to do it, almost always under conditions of an endless summer.

In the flats on the ocean side of the Keys, between land and reef, anglers fish by sight for bonefish, tarpon, permit, and many types of shark. There is some fishing to be had wading in from shore, but most anglers prefer the much greater range afforded by use of a skiff. The shallow water of the flats, ranging from 8 inches to 5 feet deep, provides a refuge for the shrimp, crabs, and juvenile fish upon which the game fish feed. In the backcountry of Florida Bay, on the Gulf side of the Keys, another world of fishing unfolds. The mangrove islands and backcountry flats of the Everglades are home to redfish, snook, sea trout, ladyfish, and amberjacks, among others.

The hiring of an experienced guide is not to be discounted in negotiating these complicated waters, although even that does not guarantee success. "You're never really on top of things," admits Marathon guide Albert Ponzoa. "With so much water out there, and with fish changing their habits on you, you're constantly learning." Yet full-time guides like Ponzoa have reached the point "where I was confident I could at least give my clients some decent chances to catch a fish."

Thanks to the multitude of bridges in the Keys, the humblest of anglers can compete for the same prize fish as the wealthy dudes with their fancy equipment and high-priced guides. Swordfish, sailfish, and tuna spend their entire lives in the open ocean, but virtually every other saltwater fish can be found hunting for food at one time or another in the tidal currents below bridges: tarpon, grouper, barracuda, snapper, amberjack, and shark, to name a few. It is not uncommon to see a whopper pulled in by Cuban yoyo—fishing line wrapped around a hand spool at one end, with a hook at the other.

To paraphrase the truism of another fishing president, Herbert Hoover, all men are equal before fish in the Conch Republic.

Hunting for Fish

Bonefish are the bullet-shaped gray ghosts of the flats; they mix in so well with the bottom that you see them for a minute, then they're gone. Tie into one and your reel starts smoking as the fish makes this screaming fast 200-yard run, suddenly stops, then starts another run before you can catch your breath.

Permit are big round fish with this black sickle tail that reflects so beautifully in the sun when they are feeding on shrimp and crabs on the bottom. They'll take your fly but they are tough characters because, one, they're big, and, two, they turn their bodies and slip-side with the current; hard as hell to bring to the boat and land.

Tarpon, you know, are very lazy, so you have to put the fly about 5 feet in front of the fish and keep it right in that window until they decide to eat it. Then we're talking a 100-pound fish—a huge animal! —chomping down on a 3-inch fly and going 4 feet out of the water like Shamu on steroids, his big eyeballs looking at you, and if you're the angler or the guide at this time, your heart jumps, too.

The ultimate Keys fishing experience is sight-fishing in the flats with a guide like Albert Ponzoa, whose above views on game fish are gleaned from fifteen years' experience guiding out of Marathon as well as fishing in the Everglades and all the way from Key Largo to Key West.

What a client should expect of any guide is good local knowledge of the conditions that affect the fishing. Fish feed with incoming and outgoing tides, and a good guide is constantly running with the tide, to be where the fish are feeding, if only for forty-five minutes, or for as long as two hours. On windy days, if a fish is sighted, the guide must be able to maneuver his boat so that the fisherman on the bow has a downwind shot at the quarry.

Ideal fishing conditions in the Keys start with a bright sun, clear blue sky, and winds no greater than 10 to 15 miles per hour. Sunlight is essential to actually seeing fish, Albert notes: "If you can't see them, you can't hunt them." Water temperature is another critical factor. "The water has to be 70 degrees or better," he says. "If it goes below 70, the fish head for deeper water and the flats become deader than Elvis." The same thing occurs if the water warms up to more than 93 degrees, as it does in the summer. "That's why the best fishing in the summer is early in the morning or later in the evening," the guide relates. "And in winter, the middle of the day is the best time to fish."

Many guides, such as Albert, provide fly-fishing or spinning tackle to anglers who have come to Florida without their own gear. Guides are also prepared to tie flies for their customers, and to offer advice on casting technique. And if they've done a good job, they expect a tip. (If your guide charges $375, a decent tip would be $50.)

In turn for all this, what does a guide expect of his client? "I expect him to try as hard as I'm trying," says Albert. "I want to see him on the bow of the boat, watching, and ready to take action. I'm disappointed in a guy who sits down after an hour because there's been no fish. But if he is the type to keep the fly rod in one hand while he eats his sandwich out of the other, and is still studying the water, I will work ten times as hard."

Above: ALBERT PONZOA CLEANS A COBIA, A FISH, COVETED BY CHEFS FOR ITS FLAVOR AND TEXTURE. MOST GAME FISH TAKEN ON THE FLATS, SUCH AS BONEFISH, PERMIT, AND TARPON, ARE CONSIDERED INEDIBLE AND ARE RELEASED AFTER BEING CAUGHT.
Opposite: GUESTS AT THE SEASCAPE RESORT IN MARATHON CAN CHILL OUT UNDER INDIGENOUS BUTTONWOOD TREES AND CONTEMPLATE THE FLATS FREQUENTED BY BASEBALL AND FLY-FISHING LEGEND TED WILLIAMS WHEN HE WAS IN PURSUIT OF BONEFISH.

REQUIEM FOR AN ANGLER

TRIBUTE TO A BELOVED BONEFISH GUIDE

O NE UNCHARACTERISTICALLY gray and forlorn January day in the Florida Keys, friends and family members said good-bye to Jimmie Albright, the legendary guide, dead at eighty-two, whose epitaph in the *New York Times* went, "Hemingway led him to blue water, and he led Herbert Hoover and Myrna Loy."

Dozens of flats skiffs, perhaps sixty in all, gathered at Bud 'n Mary's Marina on Islamorada's oceanside marinas, found the Race Channel under the bridge, turned through Bowlegs Cut on the bay side, and then motored a few miles to Buchanan Bank, one of Albright's favorite fishing destinations. It was a flotilla of local mourners, largely, many of them guides themselves who understood to what extent they owed their present livelihood to Jimmie's pioneering efforts on behalf of the fishing industry in the Keys.

Albright was born in Indiana in 1915. In 1935, he arrived in Miami, where he worked as a mate aboard an offshore charter boat, and then became a successful charter captain himself in his early twenties. He traveled to Bimini and fished for giant bluefin tuna with Ernest Hemingway. He spent a day fishing with Zane Grey aboard Grey's *Florida Lady*. When World War II began, he served overseas in the U.S. Navy, rising to the rank of lieutenant. Upon his return to the States, he moved to Islamorada and began guiding out of what was then a sleepy seashore village without electricity or running fresh water.

By improving on freshwater rods and reels, the only tackle available in the 1940s and 1950s, and pushing that tackle to its limits, Jimmie Albright helped popularize backcountry fishing and open it up to anglers all over the world. He invented the nail knot, almost universally used today by fly fishers, and a hitch called the Albright special, relied upon by saltwater anglers to securely tie lines of different diameters. He

Right and opposite: JIMMIE
ALBRIGHT'S ASHES WERE SCAT-
TERED ON BUCHANAN BANK, ONE
OF THE GUIDE'S FAVORITE FISH-
ING LOCALES, ALONG WITH FLOW-
ERS FROM MANY OF THE BOATS.

* * *

Below: IN 1956, JIMMIE, AT LEFT,
POSED WITH A TARPON HE HAD
HELPED A GRATEFUL CLIENT
FROM PHILADELPHIA LOCATE,
TIE INTO, AND LAND.

* * *

Bottom: AS BOATS DISPERSED AT
THE END OF THE SERVICE, THE
SUN BROKE THROUGH THE
CLOUDS, ADDING A HOPEFUL
NOTE TO THE SOMBER OCCASION.

and outdoor writer Joe Brooks caught the first bonefish and the first tarpon on fly tackle. They also caught the first documented sailfish on spinning tackle. And that was only the beginning of the records set by the man known as the King, or Sup, short for Super Guide.

"Some of the old-timers didn't believe that we were catching fish on fly," Albright recalled in a 1995 newspaper interview. "They doubted it, even wrote articles that we weren't doing it." But as his reputation solidified, he attracted lots of attention from the press in the 1950s and '60s. His philosophy of guiding was simple. "You've got to be able to be a teacher, a good conversationalist, and have an interest in the environment," he said. "And knowing the water and the different areas to fish." Dignitaries, movie stars, and sports heroes sought out Albright over the years to experience Florida Keys fishing with the best. He guided Jimmy Stewart and Ted Williams, with whom he became the best of friends. When Albright, battling cancer, fell upon hard financial times late in life, Williams hired a contractor to put a much-needed new roof on Albright's house. A proud man, Jimmie "blew his top" when the workmen showed up and rang his bell, a friend recalled. "He didn't know why they were there, or that Ted had arranged the whole thing."

"Jimmie and Ted were both competitive, expert, tough, and cantankerous," recalls Richard Stanczyk, owner of Bud 'n Mary's Marina in Islamorada. "Jimmie had a great sense of humor, but he was also very dedicated and disciplined. He took his guiding seriously, and helped make the industry a legitimate profession."

In spite of illness, Albright managed to catch a sailfish during the Over the Hill Sailfish Tournament in Islamorada the year before he died, winning his age category in the event. He was generous in sharing his knowledge; as one guide said, "He always took time to show us younger guys how to tie a knot."

On Buchanan Bank, the skiffs, using their push poles to anchor, tied up in 4 feet of water. The ceremony was brief. Their voices carrying clearly over the still water, a local clergyman spoke, and an Albright family representative delivered a short eulogy. Then the ashes of the deceased were scattered on the water of Florida Bay along with a wreath. There was a heavy silence, after which boats began to move away at an idle. But when they reached a respectful distance, engines roared powerfully, one after another. And the sun came out.

4
ON THE STREAM

WHEN TROUT UNLIMITED, celebrating its thirtieth anniversary, decided to name America's 100 best trout streams, it relied on the best angler-writers it could find to make the nominations, then concluded it was all very subjective anyway.

"There should be little doubt as to the finest stream," the editors declared. "It flows through paper birches and fern; through lodgepole pines and sagebrush; through the sounds of drumming grouse and the smells of a tamarack swamp. You drive there after work; you fly there every summer. It is where you caught your first trout; it's where your children will catch theirs. It is your stream, and it's the best trout stream in America."

But as proud and proprietary as fishermen may feel about their own favorite fishing spots, there are far too many rivers in America for any single angler ever to know all of them and to say which is good, better, or best. New York State alone had about 17,000 rivers and streams at last count. Apropos the semantic distinction between rivers and streams, Art Lee, a practiced and eloquent interpreter of the sport, usefully observes: "If I can't comfortably cast across it, it's a river; if I can, it's a stream."

Much more significant than width

> **PERHAPS FISHING IS, FOR ME, ONLY AN EXCUSE TO BE NEAR RIVERS. IF SO, I'M GLAD I THOUGHT OF IT.**
>
> —*Roderick L. Haig-Brown*

as a factor affecting the quality of the fish habitat is where the water in rivers and streams originates. The vast majority of them are fed primarily by surface water, including rain, snowmelt, and spillage from ponds. These tend to fluctuate in water level and water temperature with changes in season and the vagaries of weather. A minority of rivers and streams, on the other hand, are fed by underground spring creeks, which tend to ensure more constancy both in water level and in temperature. Both water supplies have major consequences for the neighborhood of fishes. Yet many rivers and streams exhibit some characteristics of each major type, leading Lee to conclude: "Each river and stream is as different from the rest as human fingerprints or snowflakes. . . . There are, in fact, no two pools, riffles, or currents exactly alike, and it seems axiomatic that as you become convinced you're master of one, nature springs new and ingenious wrinkles— the fallen tree, a gravel bar, spate, or dry spell—to humble you, like sudden caprice from a trusted lover."

It is this very mutability of habitat that keeps fishing in rivers and streams from ever becoming predictable. Apart from the basic skills involved in handling rod and reel, the angler literally and figuratively wades into a host of

Opposite: ON A 9-MILE STRETCH OF THE AU SABLE RIVER IN MICHIGAN, KNOWN AS THE "HOLY WATER," THE RIVER IS SO SHALLOW AND THE CURRENT IS SO GENTLE THAT THE ANGLER CAN WADE TO THE CENTER AND CAST EFFORTLESSLY TO EACH BANK.

natural phenomena in seeking a prize fish. "A trout stream points backward to geology and atmosopherics, to history and evolution," writes Ted Leeson in *The Habit of Rivers*, "it leads forward to insects and fish, to hydrology and botany, to literature and philosophy." To which the lowbrow bait fisherman might answer by pointing to the slogan on his T-shirt: "Fillet and release!" But even if one pooh-poohs the rhetoric, and there is much of it afloat, about the spirituality in fishing, and refuses to interest himself in the customs and traditions of a river, the pagan angler still must come to terms with the physical features of the habitat and the likely behavior of the fish in that habitat, to proceed on his quest in a logical, orderly fashion—to give method to his madness.

Some fishermen hike miles into the wilderness to find the places where they can fish in complete solitude; indeed, the remote tributaries of rivers offer adventures in small-fish angling not possible on the mother ship. Yet the healthy large river closer to home, imprinted with human history, offers as much food for thought as for fish. The ecosystem of the river has its parallel in the human society that comes to its banks: the river people.

Matt Supinski, who guides for anglers out of his own lodge, the Gray Drake, on the Muskegon River in Michigan, has fished and written extensively about the historic Pere Marquette River, which flows into Lake Michigan in the north-central part of that state. "The evolution of a river is a complex process shaped by events that occur with the changing balance of natural interaction," he writes in his *River Journal: Pere Marquette*. "Humans perhaps play the most important role in determining a river's destiny."

Down through time, the river people of the Pere Marquette have included: the Indians, the missionary-explorers, the fur trappers, the loggers, and, in modern times, the anglers, canoeists, hikers, campers, bird-watchers, and assorted other ecotourists. The angling community, however, remains the most significant presence on the Pere Marquette, drawn by the nearly year-round presence of fish, whether brown trout, chinook salmon, or steelhead trout. Like another famous Michigan river, the Au Sable, the aquatic and terrestrial insect life on the Pere Marquette is astonishingly rich and diverse, so it is a magnet for fly fishermen and an inspiration for flytiers. Fishing rivers tend to hatch their own craft as well as their own entomology. On the Pere Marquette, a double-ended drift boat has evolved with

Above: SCOTT JONES, A GUIDE WITH JOHNSON'S PERE MARQUETTE LODGE, AND HIS FRIEND BART SINANIS, OF NORFOLK, VIRGINIA, SHOW OFF ONE OF A DOZEN WILD CHINOOK SALMON THEY CAUGHT ON A BUSY DAY DURING THE MASSIVE UPSTREAM MIGRATION OF THE SPECIES, WHICH USUALLY BEGINS SHORTLY AFTER LABOR DAY EVERY YEAR. ANGLERS ON MICHIGAN'S PERE MARQUETTE RIVER ARE ENCOURAGED NOT TO TARGET SPAWNING PAIRS OF THE FISH.

a pronounced shear, permitting the oarsman to spin the boat on its axis. On the Au Sable, the boat of record is a long, low, flat-bottomed skiff, drawing mere inches of water to negotiate this much shallower river without going aground under the weight of angler and guide.

Supinski's guidebook introduces readers to Michigan river guides old and young: Zimmy Nolph, in his eighties, who guided for wealthy corporate types from Ford and Chrysler and who lamented the introduction of Pacific salmon in the 1960s, blaming that aggressive interloper for "shifting the streambeds, banks, and gravel areas around like kids in a sandbox," and Jim and Tom Johnson, transplants from Ohio who opened Johnson's Pere Marquette Lodge on the river, along with one of the best fly shops in the state. The Johnson brothers represent "the new age of river people," according to Supinski, "enthusiastic and optimistic, who after more than a decade here still feel like they've barely scratched the surface of a multidimensional watershed."

Like many of the most popular fishing rivers in America, the Pere Marquette and its branches are dotted with fishing cabins, clubs, lodges, and second homes, some dating back to the nineteenth century. There are bird dog gravestones next to a gazebo in one location, surely a sign that some form of civilization has arrived. Many of the places have became convenient references for finding fish, and their names punctuate the conversations over dinner of an evening.

On the 7-mile stretch of flies-only water established on the Pere Marquette in the 1970s, for example, one angler will tell another to "try the good pool with a nice gravel tail-out" under the iron walk bridge at the Flint Rainbow Club; or some "nice riffle-run water with hatches of Tricos and gray drakes" at Mann's Cottage, near Cedar Run; or the bigger brown trout water in the deep pools as you approach the Fin and Feather and Yellow Cottage. "The swift run near Zimmy Nolph's house holds some large browns in the summer that enjoy the deep oxygenated water," Matt advises. "Woolly Buggers fished deep will often turn a nice brown or possibly a summer steelhead."

Above: THE MADISON RIVER RUNS THROUGH SPECTACULAR BEAR TRAP CANYON IN MONTANA, WHERE THE RAPIDS ARE DESIGNATED CLASS III TO V, AND THE FISHING FOR BROWN TROUT AND RAINBOWS "ISN'T FOR THE FAINT OF HEART," SAYS OUTDOOR WRITER JOHN ROSS. GUIDES TAKE ANGLERS DOWN THE RIVER IN DRIFT BOATS, PULLING ASHORE WHENEVER THEY SPOT FISHY WATER WHERE THE CLIENTS CAN WADE IN AFTER THEIR PREY.

Of course, visiting fishermen aren't free to drop in on the owners of these many beguiling streamside habitations with their funny names and welcoming porches. Michigan law allows anglers to fish through private property so long as they stay in the stream, except when they must step ashore to circumvent obstructions. Some landowners go so far as to hire off-duty cops to patrol the banks with walkie-talkies, to keep the riffraff in the riffle, so to speak.

Like a golf course with houses along its fairways, rivers like the Pere Marquette, with park benches and wooden docks on their banks, create the illusion that the running waters have been tamed. Yet for all its signs of human settlement, "even the most tamed and domesticated river is still a wild thing," writes Ted Leeson, "and, like all wild things, must be waited out."

The waiting game depends as much on the fisherman as on the fish. "Classic waters evolve with the seasoning of an angler," Matt Supinski observes. "As one desires intimacy with the river, the lady of the river reveals herself and hides on her whims, not necessarily on your terms of yearning and desire."

A local conservation group, the Pere Marquette Watershed Council, works with property owners and state and federal agencies to preserve the health and integrity of the river basin. The nonprofit Conservation Resource Alliance, founded in 1968, coordinates natural resource stewardship on a regional level. The Pere Marquette is one of ten "blue-ribbon trout streams" in its river care program in a thirteen-county region in northern Michigan, designed to "guarantee that natural resource professionals maintain a consistent action plan for each river."

The river, named after Father Jacques Marquette, the French Jesuit missionary who explored the region with Louis Joliet in the 1600s, holds a special fascination for students of angling history in America. It was once a grayling stream, but the graylings, members of the salmon family, died out following decades of massive logging beginning in the 1850s, which leeched harmful sediments into their habitat. In time the water cleared and the river purged itself of toxins, at which point brown trout from the Black Forest region of Germany were successfully introduced into the river in 1884, the first such planting in North America. The next year, rainbow trout fingerlings from California were brought in, but they mysteriously disappeared. It turned out that the trout were actually a catchall of migrating steelhead trout strains; the missing steelhead had simply migrated downriver into Lake Michigan, where they would feed and fatten up until the spawning instinct returned them to the river. Today, healthy brown trout, rainbows, and steelhead, the last-named described by one Michigan angler as "acrobatic freight trains when hooked," help to ensure interesting fishing on the P.M. almost year-round.

Yet another migrating species was planted in the 1960s, Chinook salmon from the Pacific, and these too have thrived in the watershed. "Chinook usually congregate in Lake Michigan at the mouth of the Pere Marquette in August," reports Supinski. "When salmon are in, the river is a madhouse of crazed anglers looking for their trophy of a lifetime."

Above: A HUNTING AND FISHING LICENSE WAS CONSIDERED "A DOCUMENT OF HONOR" IN THE MONTANA OF THE 1930S. THE TOWN OF LIVINGSTON, WHERE THE TAXIDERMIST WHO RECEIVED THIS LICENSE RESIDED, IS STILL A MECCA FOR WESTERN SPORTSMEN.

* * *

Opposite: THE FLYING A RANCH IN PINEDALE, WYOMING, IS A SMALL, FAMILY-RUN COMPOUND OF HANDCRAFTED LOG CABINS DATING FROM 1929, RESTORED AND FURNISHED WITH HANDMADE NATIVE PINE CHAIRS, TABLES, AND BEDS. GUESTS CAN FISH FOR RAINBOW AND BROOK TROUT IN ONE OF TWO LARGE STREAM-FED PONDS OR HIRE A GUIDE TO TACKLE NEARBY MOUNTAIN LAKES AND STREAMS OR THE SLIGHTLY MORE AWESOME SNAKE AND GREEN RIVERS.

* * *

Overleaf: THE GREEN RIVER OFFERS SPECTACULAR VIEWS, AND SUPERIOR TROUT FISHING, FROM SOUTHWESTERN WYOMING INTO NORTHERN UTAH.

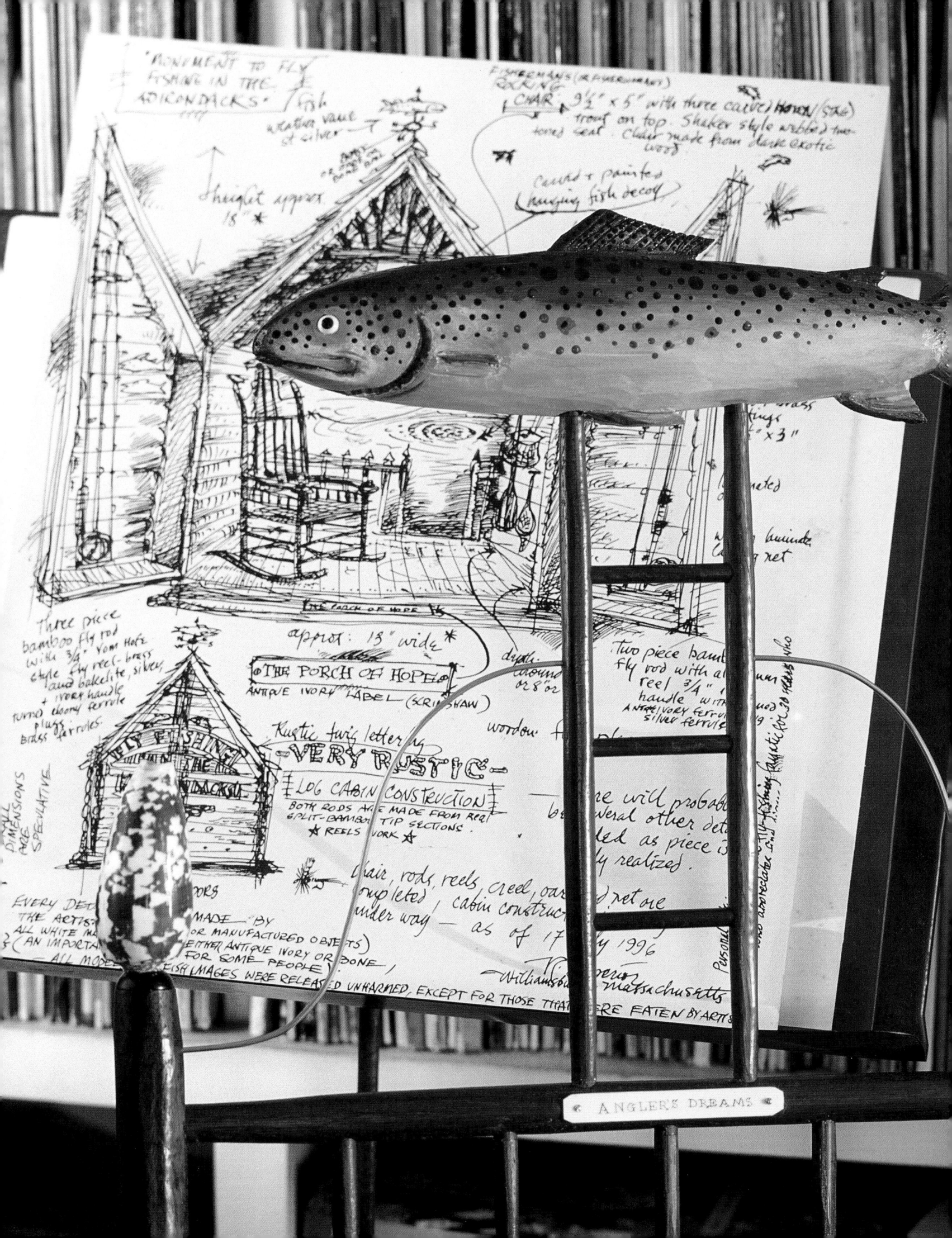

TWO SCHOOLS OF FISH

SUPERIOR WORKMANSHIP IN PORCELAIN AND WOOD

EVEN THOUGH their chosen mediums are material worlds apart, artists Roy and Mara Superior both use fish as a recurring theme in their work, and that is immediately clear to any visitor to the couple's home in Williamsburg, Massachusetts.

Roy studied illustration, painting, and printmaking at the Pratt Institute and Yale University, but he gravitated to working in wood and now heads the wood department at the Philadelphia College of Art. In teaching woodcraft to others, he preaches tradition over convenience. "Make yourself a nice small mallet," he urges, "because it feels better than the ones you can buy." Or "Use antique C-clamps for securing wood on the table saw; they're more aesthetic."

Although he occasionally builds conventional furniture, like chairs or a sideboard, Roy's abiding passion is miniature forms. "It started almost out of necessity," he says. "We had moved to Massachusetts, and while on a sabbatical from teaching, I renovated our house and built my studio, which left us broke but with lots of small pieces of wood. Actu-

ally, I had already made a couple of small jewelry boxes, and I liked working on that scale." At about the same time, his father, a dentist, had died, and Roy found among his possessions several jars full of wood dowels. "I think they were used, with cotton wrapped around them, as dental swabs. They were only $3/32$ inch in diameter, and it occurred to me they would make great miniature pegs for furniture."

The found objects of his

Opposite: ROY SUPERIOR'S ANGLER'S DREAM, A FULL-SIZED ROCKING CHAIR OF PADOUK, AN EXOTIC WOOD FOUND ON ISLANDS IN THE INDIAN OCEAN, TOPPED WITH CARVED WOOD TROUT, WAS INSPIRED BY A MINIATURE CHAIR HE MADE FOR A CONSTRUCTION, *MONUMENT TO FLY FISHING,* IN 1995. THAT CHAIR CAN BE SEEN IN THE WORKING DRAWING FOR THE CONSTRUCTION, WHICH AT THE TIME HE MADE THE DRAWING WAS CALLED *THE PORCH OF HOPE.*

* * *

Above: THE 1828 GREEK REVIVAL HOUSE IN WESTERN MASSACHU-SETTS IS TEN MINUTES FROM ROY'S FAVORITE STREAM, THE DEERFIELD RIVER.

* * *

Left: ONE CORNER OF ROY'S WORKSHOP IS RESERVED FOR FLY-FISHING GEAR.

Below: ROY SUPERIOR FASHIONED
THIS WALKING STICK WITH THE
FISH-SHAPED HANDLE OUT OF
APPLEWOOD, AND CHIP-CARVED
THE CANE WITH "SO LITTLE
TIME, SO MANY FISH."

* * *

Bottom: MARA SUPERIOR'S
FAVORITE PORCELAINS ARE DIS-
PLAYED IN A CABINET BUILT
BY HER HUSBAND.

fishing passion make their way into his work as well. A piece he completed in 1995, *Monument to Fly Fishing*, for example, measures only 23 by 20 by 20 inches, but conveys a piscatorial universe. Made of wood, bone, and the synthetic Corian, the tiny rustic cabin invites the observer to look through an interior packed with miniature fishing paraphernalia out to a painted lake where a fish has just risen. Hanging on the cabin doors are profiles of fish Roy has caught and two miniature fly rods with reels that actually work.

Mara knows for a fact that friends and relatives of anglers are regular customers for her fish pieces, but all her work is a favorite of collectors. It is represented in the White House Collection of American Crafts and the permanent collection of the Smithsonian Institution's Renwick Gallery, as is Roy's work. Mara spends the winter building her ceramic pieces. During the summer and early fall, she paints and glazes the pieces for three or four final kiln firings.

"This is the nervous-making time for me," she admits. Mara loads fifteen to twenty pieces into each kiln and fires it to the highest termperature the clay can withstand—a few more degrees and it would begin to melt into blobs of glass. She makes subtle adjustments to the atmosphere inside in response to the color and shape of the flames and the smoke the kiln is producing. If the adjustments are correct, and she maintains the delicate balance of oxygen and carbon dioxide, her porcelain remains white, her glaze becomes clear, and painted colors are brilliant. In particular, she seeks to create blushing copper reds. If she misses by a little, they go black, but when they come out right, as they usually do, the result is porcelain pushed precisely to its limits.

Above: ALTHOUGH NO TWO ARE
IDENTICAL, MARA SUPERIOR'S
HAND-PAINTED, SLAB-BUILT
PORCELAIN PLATTERS FRE-
QUENTLY BEAR THE IMAGE OF A
SALMON, STRIPED BASS, OR
TROUT, "BECAUSE THEY HAVE
BEEN SUCH A PREVALENT
IMAGE IN THE HOUSE," SHE
EXPLAINS. "THE MYSTERIOUS
CHARACTER AND ALLURE OF
THOSE FISH, AS I CAME TO
UNDERSTAND THEIR SPECIAL
QUALITIES THROUGH ROY,
INTRIGUED ME, AND NOW MY
SALMON PLATTER, FOR INSTANCE,
HAS BECOME ONE OF MY
PERENNIAL PIECES."

* * *

Left: OLIVER, A SPRINGER
SPANIEL, LOLLS ABOUT IN A ROOM
DEVOTED TO BOOKS AND MUSIC;
ROY SUPERIOR PLAYS BOTH THE
CLARINET AND SOPRANO
SAXOPHONE, BUT EVER SINCE
BECOMING A COMMITTED
FLY FISHERMAN, HE FORSAKES
HIS MUSIC AT THE END OF A WORK
SESSION IN THE STUDIO FOR A
TRIP TO THE DEERFIELD RIVER,
"BUT NEVER MORE THAN ONCE
A DAY," HE INSISTS.

HAUNTED BY RIVERS

FAMILY RANCH ON THE PERE MARQUETTE

That *First Casting Must Be Good* is the title of George W. Cannon's autobiography, but even though Cannon was an avid trout fisherman, the title does not refer to fly casting. It is simply the philosophy that the author followed in starting an iron foundry with two partners in Muskegon, Michigan, in 1908. So successful was his approach to casting metal that the company grew and prospered for more than half a century, eventually to become the nation's largest independent foundry, finally being sold to Textron, Inc., in 1956.

Yet it is as a fisherman as much as a business leader that Cannon's children and grandchildren remember him, such was his passion for the sport. He gave angling the same single-minded attention as he did his business affairs. To entertain friends and important customers of the foundry, the company built Hearthstone, a fishing lodge on the Pere Marquette River, some 70 miles from Muskegon, in 1927. "While other executives did the entertaining at the lodge," George W. Cannon Jr. recalls, "my father fished on weekends from sunup to sundown, and came to know every bend and logjam in the river. Fish were plentiful then, and he sent the less successful visitor home from Hearthstone with warm memories and an iced container that held two to four big, fine trout."

When a much larger log dwelling on an extended stretch of the river became available, the senior Cannon leaped at the chance to buy it for his family retreat. He

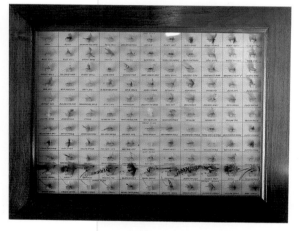

Opposite: THE LIFE-SIZED PORTRAIT OF GEORGE W. CANNON WAS PAINTED BY ONE OF HIS DAUGHTERS, BEE NICHOLLS, IN THE 1950S, AFTER A FAVORITE PHOTOGRAPH OF THE ANGLER.

Above: A REPRESENTATIVE SAMPLING OF TROUT FLIES RUNS FROM ADAM TO YELLOW SALLY. LONG CONSIDERED ONE OF THE FINEST HATCH-MATCHING RIVERS IN THE COUNTRY, THE PERE MARQUETTE AQUATIC INSECT POPULATION IS ACTUALLY ON THE INCREASE.

* * *

Left: A DRAWING COMMISSIONED BY CANNON INCLUDED A ROAD MAP FOR GUESTS TO FOLLOW TO RIVER RANCH, AND ILLUSTRATED SOME ACTIVITIES THEY MIGHT ENJOY ONCE THEY GOT THERE.

Left: JOHN CINKA, A GUIDE WITH JOHNSON'S PERE MARQUETTE LODGE, PROBES A RUN ALONG THE BANKS OF THE RIVER, NOT FAR FROM RIVER RANCH. LIKE OTHER CONSERVATION-MINDED SETTLERS ON THE PERE MARQUETTE, GEORGE W. CANNON TRIED TO IMPROVE THE FISHING QUALITY OF THE RIVER BY PROTECTING ITS BANKS WITH CABLED LOGS, STUMPS, AND ROCKS.

* * *

Below: THE TACKLE HOUSE AT RIVER RANCH IS STOCKED WITH SPINNING AND FLY-FISHING TACKLE, WADERS, FISHING VESTS, AND ANY OTHER GEAR A VISITOR MIGHT NEED TO TRY HIS OR HER LUCK ON THE RIVER.

* * *

Bottom: IF THE RIVER OUTING IS UNSUCCESSFUL, THERE IS ALWAYS THE FISHERMAN'S CRYING TOWEL TO TURN TO FOR COMFORT.

named it River Ranch. It had been built in the 1920s by a fishing friend, Robert W. Irwin, founder of the Irwin Furniture Company in Grand Rapids, Michigan, then one of the nation's leading fine furniture makers. Irwin had spared no expense in creating a full-service fishing compound with its own tackle and equipment log cabin, fishing docks, and an electric generating plant, in the then remote rural area.

Anglers began to settle on the Pere Marquette—or, in local parlance, the P.M.—as early as the 1880s. The oldest surviving club in the area is the Kinne Creek Club, established in 1888. The Pere Marquette Rod & Gun Club, founded on March 10, 1916, still exists as a sprawling compound of family-owned camps and lodges perched on wooded bluffs overlooking the river, filled with mementos of hunting and fishing.

Expansion on the river continued into the 1920s. The Pere Marquette Railroad provided access to the river from Ludington, at its mouth, and from the eastern part of the state. And the vast new wealth generated by the automotive industry in Detroit, the furniture industry in Grand Rapids, and allied fields of business in the state provided the discretionary income needed for splurging on such luxuries as fishing camps and wilderness retreats.

Under George Cannon, the tackle house at River Ranch was expanded, a three-hole golf course was laid out on the grounds, and a guest house overlooking the river was added. He also worked to improve the fishing quality of the river, shoring up banks with cabled logs, stumps, and rocks. He took particular delight in teaching young people to fish, according to George Jr., and spent many happy extended days on the river, fishing up to age ninety with friends and longtime local guides Graham MacDougall, Zimmy Nolph, and others. Since then, several generations of the Cannon family continue to enjoy the angler's haven of River Ranch.

UP IN MICHIGAN

SMALL TOWNS AND BIG TWO-HEARTED RIVERS

IT HASN'T CHANGED and we don't want it to," says Tom Symons, whose grandfather built "the Cabin," as it was always marked on old county maps, on the Au Sable River in central Michigan in 1903. "There's never been a telephone, and as far as I'm concerned, there never will be."

The Au Sable River itself, one of the largest ground spring rivers in North America, consists of four branches, the east, middle, north, and south. Private cabins, permanent residences, and hunting and fishing lodges have proliferated along all its tributaries. The cabin built by Symons's grandfather, Charles Kuehl, a well-to-do Saginaw lumberman, is located on the north branch. It's a place where the only competition for the lure of the stream comes from the works of Rudyard Kipling and Frank Norris, gathering dust on bookshelves, or of two writers of more recent vintage whose lives and careers were shaped by their experience of fishing on Michigan rivers: Ernest Hemingway and the less well known John D. Voelker.

Hemingway fished a number of rivers and streams in Michigan as a teenager, including the Boardman, Pigeon, Black, Sturgeon, and Fox. His experience on the Fox River was the basis for one of his most famous short stories, "Big Two-Hearted River," which he wrote in Paris in 1924. In the summer of 1916, he and a young friend, Lewis Clarahan, took a steamer from Chicago to the Traverse City area of Michigan, then hiked for ten days, fishing every day along the way, to the cottage of family friends on Walloon Lake, near Petoskey. Hemingway's handwritten diary of the trip, published in *The American Fly Fisher* in 1989, reveals a precocious, writerly attention to detail, a nose for people and places that might provide, as he put it, "good stuff for stories & essays," and, above all, a passion for fishing.

Voelker was an attorney in private practice and a Michigan Supreme Court justice for many years, who achieved national celebrity in 1958 with the best-seller *Anatomy of a Murder*, which he wrote under the pen name Robert Traver. Like Hemingway, Voelker had a powerful affinity for fishing, in his case on Michigan's wild Upper Peninsula, and he gained some degree of prominence writing about the characters, human and otherwise, who inhabited that world. He

Opposite: A CLASSIC FAMILY CAMP ON THE AU SABLE RIVER HAS A PORCH THAT TAKES ADVANTAGE OF THE VIEW. LIKE THE PERE MARQUETTE AND OTHER RIVERS IN WESTERN AND NORTHERN MICHIGAN, THE AU SABLE HAS NUMEROUS HOUSES, COTTAGES, AND CABINS ALONG ITS BANKS, BUT MOST OF THEM ARE DISCREETLY SITED SO AS TO PRESERVE AN ATMOSPHERE OF THE WILD ON THE RIVER ITSELF.

* * *

Below: MICHIGAN RIVER TOWNS LIKE BALDWIN AND GRAYLING BOAST NUMEROUS COMMERCIAL ENTERPRISES THEMED TO THE SPORT OF ANGLING.

Right: "IF YOU WERE A FLY FISH-
ERMAN AND COULD CREATE A
PERFECT ENVIRONMENT FOR
YOUR SPORT, THE AU SABLE
WOULD BE IT," SAYS AN ADMIT-
TEDLY BIASED RUSTY GATES,
OWNER OF THE GATES AU SABLE
LODGE DIRECTLY ON THE RIVER.
WADING TO THE CENTER OF THE
STREAM, THE ANGLER CAN CAST
7 OR 8 FEET TO HIT BOTH BANKS.
THE RIVER BOTTOM IS A FINE
PEA GRAVEL AND THE WATER
LEVEL NEVER VARIES BY MORE
THAN 6 INCHES.

* * *

Top: RUSTY GATES AND HIS
GOLDEN RETRIEVER, HOLLY, OUT-
SIDE THE FLY SHOP.

* * *

Above: RUSTY GATES'S BROTHER,
JIM, WHO RETIRED AFTER TEACH-
ING IN ALASKA FOR TWENTY-FIVE
YEARS, HAS SIGNED ON TO GUIDE
ANGLERS AND HELP IN OTHER
ROLES AT THE LODGE. HERE HE IS
FISHING IN FRONT OF AN OLD
BOATHOUSE, ORIGINALLY USED TO
STORE THE AU SABLE BOAT.

Top left: DURING INACTIVE PERIODS ON THE RIVER, ANGLERS GATHER IN THE SHOP AT GATES AU SABLE LODGE TO COMPARE NOTES, WATCH RUSTY TIE FLIES, AND STRATEGIZE THEIR NEXT FISHING OUTINGS.

* * *

Center left: THE AU SABLE GUIDE-BOAT IS DESIGNED TO CARRY THE WEIGHT OF TWO ADULTS, ANGLER AND GUIDE, WITHOUT GOING AGROUND IN A RIVER AS SHALLOW AS 6 INCHES IN SOME PLACES.

* * *

Bottom left: IN ORDER TO PROVIDE HABITAT AND COVER FOR FISH—"TROUT HOTELS," AS RUSTY GATES CALLS THEM—CREWS WORK FROM MAY THROUGH OCTOBER CREATING STRUCTURE OUT OF NATURAL MATERIALS SUCH AS FALLEN CEDARS (IN LOCAL PARLANCE, "CEDAR SWEEPERS") ALL ALONG THE RIVER. WITHOUT SUCH PROTECTION, THE TROUT IN ANY SHALLOW RIVER WOULD MAKE EASY PREY FOR HAWKS AND OTHER RAPTORS, SAYS GATES.

wrote three fishing books: the particularly well received *Trout Madness,* then *Anatomy of a Fisherman,* and *Trout Magic.*

If Hemingway and Voelker-Traver are Michigan's most notable angler-writers, the Au Sable is its most famous trout stream. As Elizabeth Edwards noted in *Traverse* magazine, "When the talk turns to trout fishing in Michigan, the Au Sable invariably runs through it." Rising west of the old logging town of Grayling, the river flows cool and clear over cobble bottom with the prolific insect life to sustain up to 4,000 trout per mile. In one stretch east of town, the currents are so gentle and so shallow that an angler can wade to the center and cast effortlessly to both banks. Or one can take one's seat at the front of an elegant Au Sable riverboat, which guides pole up and down the river on floating fishing trips that last as long as eight to ten hours.

The conservationist organization Trout Unlimited, now 450 chapters strong nationwide, was conceived in the home of George A. Griffith on the banks of the Au Sable in 1959. Years later, TU parted ways with local conservationists who wanted to institute a catch-and-release policy along the Holy Water. The locals, led by Rusty Gates and his own organization, the Anglers of the Au Sable, prevailed, and now, thanks to that policy, the resident browns grow big, fat, and old. For his efforts Rusty was named Angler of the Year by *Fly Rod and Reel* magazine in 1995.

Gates, like his father before him, is owner and operator of Gates Au Sable Lodge, a cozy motel-style inn so close to the river a guest could cast into it from one of the rooms. Rusty's wife, Julie, runs the restaurant next door, turning out homemade soups, pies, and breads. The adjoining fly shop is where Rusty presides over the reservations book, fields questions from anglers from fifty states and all walks of life, and ties flies by the thousands.

Above: ALTHOUGH GOURMET BANQUETS WERE NOT A TRADITION IN THIS RIVER HOUSE, ITS CAMP KITCHEN HAS ALL THE TOOLS REQUIRED TO MAKE THE CATCH OF THE DAY AS APPETIZING AS POSSIBLE.

* * *

Left: A NATIVE STONE FIREPLACE AND RUSTIC FURNISHINGS GIVE "THE CABIN" A TIMELESS SPORTING AMBIENCE. TOM SYMONS, GRANDSON OF CHARLES KUEHL AND THE CABIN'S PRESENT OWNER, SAYS THAT HIS WIFE, LYNN, CLAIMS SHE HAS CAUGHT EVERY BROOK TROUT IN FRONT OF THE PLACE SEVERAL TIMES OVER.

Hemingway and Traver

Two Michigan anglers, Ernest Hemingway, an innocent at seventeen, and Robert Traver, the curmudgeon in his maturity, revealed the spring and autumn of the fisherman's soul in the following excerpts from their work. Hemingway's diary, *Hike to Walloon Lake, June 10–21, 1916*, recounts a fishing trip he made with a friend from Chicago to northern Michigan. Traver, the pen name of John D. Voelker, wrote his *Testament of a Fisherman* late in his life.

"Thurs. We broke camp and hiked to Mayfield. We said so long to some old folks that we traded the two suckers to for a quart of milk. The old woman smoked a pipe. The old man is 78 yrs. and the woman 85. They were delighted with the suckers. We went from Mayfield to Walton Junction (the place that put the junk in junction) and where we met the train & then went to Kalkaska. We hiked from there to Rug a little place on Rapid River. Its a creek about the size of Hortons with many deep holes. Also two nice dams. We fished from 4 to 5 and Lew caught one nice rainbow and a brook trout and I caught three rainbows. We camped on a high hill. There is a small water power elecric plant out here in the wildnerness run by a fellow from Chicago. He had a rainbow 20 inches long.

"Friday. It rained hard last night. We got up early in the morning and fished. Lew lost a whale of a rainbow just below the power plant. I caught ten brook trout and Lew caught nine. Certainly was glad to get our mail at Kalkaska. Lew caught two that would weigh about a pound apiece. We got our dinner cooked (bacon) and were just starting to fry the big rainbow when a thunderstorm came up and we had to go into the tent. We took some dandy pictures of the Rapid River . . ."

—Ernest Hemingway's diary, June 10–21, 1916

"I fish because I love to; because I love the environs where trout are found, which are invariably beautiful, and hate the environs where crowds of people are found, which are invariably ugly; because of all the television commercials, cocktail parties, and assorted social posturing I thus escape; because, in a world where most men seem to spend their lives doing things they hate, my fishing is at once an endless source of delight and an act of small rebellion; because trout do not lie or cheat and cannot be bought or bribed or impressed by power, but respond only to quietude and humility and endless patience; because I suspect that men are going along this way for the last time, and I for one don't want to waste the trip; because mercifully there are no telephones on trout waters; because only in the woods can I find solitude without loneliness; because bourbon out of an old tin cup always tastes better out there; because maybe one day I will catch a mermaid; and, finally, not because I regard fishing as being so terribly important but because I suspect that so many of the other concerns of men are equally unimportant—and not nearly so much fun."

—Robert Traver, *Testament of a Fisherman*

Above: WEATHER-BEATEN CHAIRS LEFT OUT ALONG THE HOLY WATER SECTION OF THE AU SABLE RIVER IN MICHIGAN OFFER A PLACE FROM WHICH TO PUT THE SPORT OF ANGLING, AND PERHAPS LIFE ITSELF, IF ONE IS INQUISITIVE ABOUT SUCH THINGS, INTO PERSPECTIVE. *Opposite:* SLEEPING PLATFORMS IN THE SYMONS CABIN, WITHIN EARS' REACH OF THE RIVER, ENSURE RESTFUL NIGHTS FOR VISITING FISHERMEN.

ANGLING FOR ANTIQUES

A FISHERMAN'S ONE-ROOM SCHOOLHOUSE

WHEN MANHATTAN angler-actor-restaurateur Craig Bero wants to get away from it all, he knows exactly where to do it: in a converted one-room schoolhouse off the beaten path in upstate New York, not far from a country stream he also likes to call his own.

"The building dates from the 1850s and it was last used as a classroom in the 1948–49 school year," he explains, pointing to initials legible to this day carved into the walls years ago by kids. The retreat still serves as an educational facility of sorts: it is filled with books, paintings, carvings, and other objects that provide a veritable primer on the the history and traditions of angling in Great Britain and America. Early English fly rods and reels, butterfly bass flies created by milliner Frances Stearns for L.L. Bean in the 1930s, and mementos of the area in northern Wisconsin where Craig grew up, including colorful ice jigging sticks painted and carved by Winnebago Indians in the 1920s, all commingle cheerfully within a house that is as much a stage set as it is a residence.

A traditionalist to the core, Craig gets a kick out of pursuing the old way of doing things, whether it's fishing with antique tackle, or cross-country skiing on early Nordic gear: "I got to see wood going through the snow." At times it seems as if he is bent on reproducing all that meant the most to him when he was a child in Algoma, population 1,200 back then, on the Door Peninsula, between the sheltered waters of Green Bay, to the west, and the vast expanse of Lake Michigan to the east, learning so much of what he knows today about the crafts of woods and water from Potawatomi and Menominee tribe members who had befriended him.

For example, Craig spent one recent summer in the

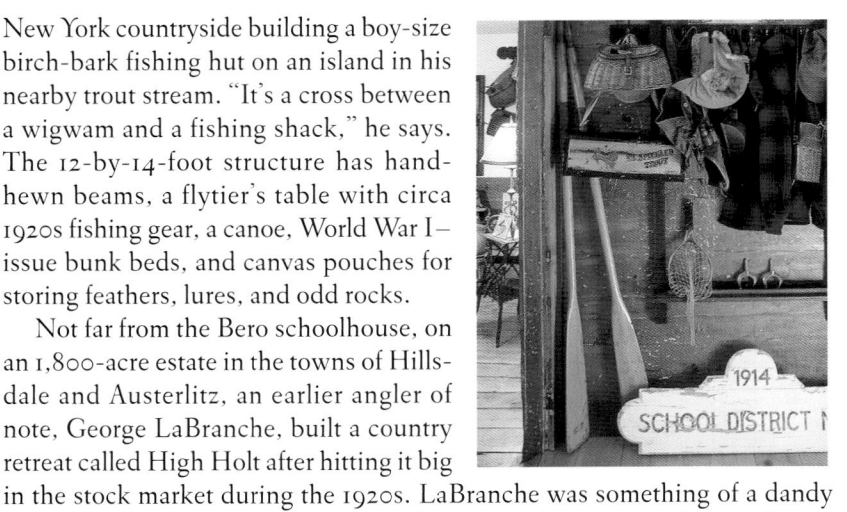

New York countryside building a boy-size birch-bark fishing hut on an island in his nearby trout stream. "It's a cross between a wigwam and a fishing shack," he says. The 12-by-14-foot structure has hand-hewn beams, a flytier's table with circa 1920s fishing gear, a canoe, World War I–issue bunk beds, and canvas pouches for storing feathers, lures, and odd rocks.

Not far from the Bero schoolhouse, on an 1,800-acre estate in the towns of Hillsdale and Austerlitz, an earlier angler of note, George LaBranche, built a country retreat called High Holt after hitting it big in the stock market during the 1920s. LaBranche was something of a dandy both on and off stream, wearing vest, collar, and tie and the Sherlock Holmes–like helmet type of fishing hat, according to *Esquire* magazine founder and angler Arnold Gingrich, but he was a masterful fly fisherman and "the outstanding exponent and advocate of the dry fly at the height of its vogue in America." He wrote two pioneering tomes on the subject: *The Dry Fly and Fast Water,* 1914, and *The Salmon and the Dry Fly,* 1924.

Bringing up from Manhattan tins of Melachrino cigarettes and bootleg gin for his guests, and dining on pheasant and salmon, LaBranche probably enjoyed his creature comforts at High Holt too much to have found Craig Bero's humble fishing camp to his liking, but perhaps the two anglers, die-hard traditionalists yet stubbornly eclectic in their tastes, would have found common ground on the stream.

Above: THE REINFORCED STEEL
AND CONCRETE CASTING OF A
LEAPING TROUT IN TURBULENT
WATER WAS MADE AROUND 1890
AND WAS PROBABLY USED AS A
DECORATIVE ELEMENT IN A NEW
YORK CITY WATER FOUNTAIN.
CREELS ON THE WALL INCLUDE A
HORIZONTAL SLAT CREEL WITH A
CENTER HOLE FROM WISCONSIN,
A TURTLE CREEL WITH A CARVED
TURTLE LATCH, AND A WOVEN
ALUMINUM CREEL, MADE AFTER
WORLD WAR II.

* * *.

Left: AN OLD TIN MATCH HOLDER
WITH AN ANGLING THEME MIGHT
HAVE GRACED A FISHERMAN'S
CABIN IN THE DEEP WOODS.

THE REEL THING

RESTORING THE SHINE TO VINTAGE TACKLE

HOAGY BIX CARMICHAEL cast his first fishing line on the waters of a swimming pool on Sunset Boulevard in Hollywood, where his father, the legendary songwriter Hoagy Carmichael ("Stardust," "Up a Lazy River," "Georgia on My Mind"), had moved from Indiana in furtherance of his show business career. (He is named after his father and one of his father's best friends, the jazz cornetist Bix Beiderbecke.) But he did not discover fly-fishing until 1967, during a trip to Canada for the world's fair. "I couldn't catch a thing," he recalls, "but I really caught the bug then."

Since then Hoagy has mastered not only fly-fishing but also some of the ancient and honorable crafts with which it is associated. He makes bamboo fly rods, each of which takes "sixty-five hours of honest work," he estimates, and he repairs and restores antique fly reels, some of the latter being volunteer labor for the American Museum of Fly Fishing and the Catskill Fly Fishing Center and Museum. His stone house in North Salem, New York, is only minutes from the highway, providing a quick and convenient commute to Manhattan and his duties as president of Amsong, an association of songwriters and their heirs. But its hilltop location, insulated from neighbors by woods, has the feel of a remote highland redoubt. He has converted part of a barn on his property into his workshop. And, yes, there is a swimming pool, but he doesn't fish in it.

The workbench and many of the tools in the shop once belonged to Edward Everett Garrison, one of the world's finest fly rod craftsmen, whom Hoagy befriended on a fishing trip in the Catskills in 1969. Hoagy, a film and television producer—*Mister Rogers' Neighborhood* is one of his credits—documented Garrison's meticulous rod-making process in a film, *Creating the Garrison Fly Rod.* "The things that separate Garrisons from other rods," says Carmichael, "are their tapering

Opposite: PERHAPS THE MOST IMPORTANT REELS IN CARMICHAEL'S COLLECTION ARE THE DISTINCTIVELY AMERICAN BUT NOW RARELY SEEN SIDE-MOUNT FLY REELS. THE EARLIEST PATENTED AMERICAN FLY REEL WAS A SIDEMOUNT MADE BY A GUNSMITH IN ROCHESTER, NEW YORK, IN 1859. LESS THAN A DECADE LATER, ANSON HATCH OF NEW HAVEN, CONNECTICUT, SUBMITTED A REEL MODEL TO THE U.S. PATENT OFFICE ON JUNE 19, 1866, AS AN IMPROVE-MENT ON THE FIRST SIDEMOUNT WITH ITS ADDITION OF A SIDE-GUARD TO PREVENT LINE FROM BILLOWING OUT. THIS RARE PATENT MODEL, NOW MORE THAN A CENTURY OLD, STILL HAS ITS ORIGINAL HAND-LETTERED PATENT OFFICE TAG.

* * *

Right: HOAGY CRAFTS RODS AND REELS WITH THE SAME ATTEN-TION TO DETAIL THAT HIS FAMOUS FATHER, WHOSE BIRTH CENTENARY WAS CELEBRATED IN 1999, BROUGHT TO SONGWRITING.

* * *

Below: THE RAW HOLLOW WOODY CULMS, OR STALKS, OF BAMBOO FROM CHINA AWAIT THEIR PAINSTAKING TRANSFORMATION INTO A FLY ROD OF BEAUTY AND PRACTICALITY.

action, the fact that they are built to strong tolerances yet are hand-planed, and their almost monastic simplicity—they are excellent utilitarian rods that don't call attention to themselves."

According to antique tackle expert Ken Reback, Garrison was one of a hand-ful of highly respected rod makers in the post–World War II era whose output was very small but whose handiwork was considered the very epitome of the rod maker's art. Including Pinky Gillum, Paul Young, and Jim Payne in this select group, Reback observes that their rods "are both fishable and highly col-lectible, and in good condition sell for thousands of dollars." Rod makers like Paul Young developed into full-fledged business operations. Young issued his first catalog in 1925 and by the 1940s was offering twenty-nine two-piece mod-els and twenty-seven three-piece models. After his death in 1960, his son Jack and, subsequently, his grandson Todd have carried on the tradition. His legacy also survives in the craftsmanship of Bob Summers in Traverse City, Michi-gan, who made rods with the Youngs before setting out on his own in 1972.

When Garrison died in 1975, Hoagy gathered up all of Garrison's notes and equipment and began making his own rods. Editing his mentor's notes, he produced the book *A Master's Guide to Building a Bamboo Fly Rod,* which fast became the standard text in the field. Hoagy sought out and acquired some of the finest and most historic Garrison fly rods, building a definitive collection which he subsequently donated to the American Museum of Fly Fishing. At the same time, Hoagy himself became one of the most highly regarded rod craftsman of his generation, his creations selling for thousands of dollars. "It gets into you," he says of his obsession with fashioning hollow woody culms, or stalks, of bamboo from China into classic fly rods and, now, restoring antique fly reels into things of practical beauty. "I just love doing it. It's a pleasure and it's a challenge."

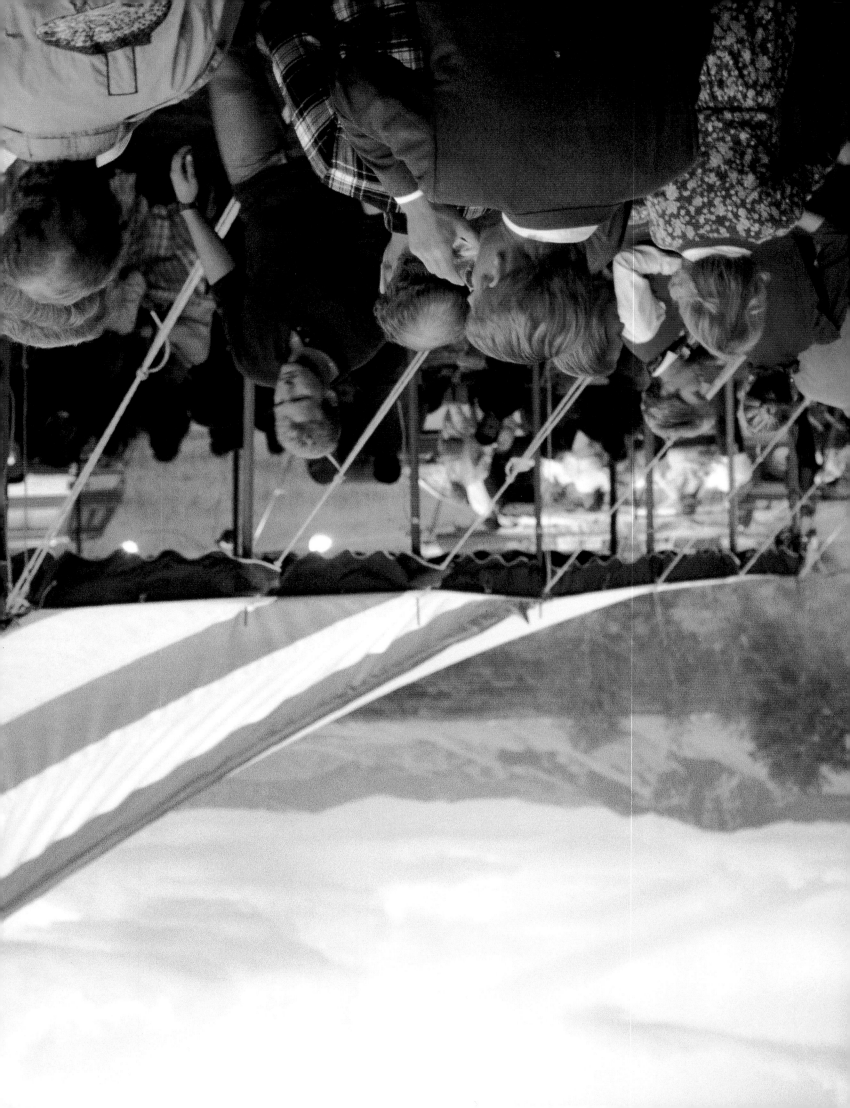

HAVE FLY, WILL TRAVEL

RAISING FISH, AND MONEY, FOR A WESTERN RIVER

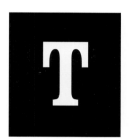

THE COUNTRYSIDE is straight out of a John Wayne movie—miles of sky, jagged peaks, lush meadows. But the fighting is done with a fly rod. It's the annual Jackson Hole One-Fly Contest on the spectacular Snake River of Wyoming, drawing fishing guides and celebrity anglers from around the world every September, and raising money, and consciousness, for a fishery that is the quintessence of the angling experience of the American West.

"The Wyoming-Idaho-Montana area of the Rocky Mountains probably offers the most consistent quality trout fishing in the world," says Tom Rosenbauer, referring to rivers such as the Yellowstone, Madison, Firehole, Henry's Fork, and Bighorn. "Besides the abundance of wild trout streams, the scenery cannot be equaled anywhere. Where else can you stand knee-deep in a river and see snowcapped peaks, then look in the other direction and see elk or bison grazing in a meadow—with steam from a geyser as a backdrop."

The One-Fly, first held in 1986, rotates contestants from thirty-six teams through eight sections of the Snake River over a period of two days. Native cutthroat trout, characterized by two orange-red slashes under the jaw, are the principal game fish in western rivers, first identified by William Clark, who collected specimens with Meriwether Lewis on the pair's famed expedition of 1804. Rainbow and brook trout are also found. The anglers fish from two-ended craft or rubber riverboats and

Opposite and below: AFTER ONE EDITION OF THE ANNUAL ONE-FLY TOURNAMENT IN JACKSON HOLE, WYOMING, PARTICIPANTS RELAXED WITH A COCKTAIL PARTY AND BARBECUE DINNER AT RIVERMEADOWS RESORT. "YOU'RE SUPPOSED TO GO FISHING TENSE AND COME BACK RELAXED,"

OBSERVED THE PROGRAM FOR THE 1999 ONE-FLY. "IF YOU COME BACK HOME A BASKET CASE, YOU'VE MISSED THE POINT."

* * *

Left: HELD ON THE SNAKE RIVER IN THE RUGGED EMBRACE OF THE TETON MOUNTAINS, THE ONE-FLY RAISES MONEY FOR WATERSHED CONSERVATION AND FLY-FISHING EDUCATION.

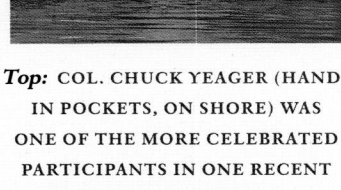

Top: COL. CHUCK YEAGER (HANDS
IN POCKETS, ON SHORE) WAS
ONE OF THE MORE CELEBRATED
PARTICIPANTS IN ONE RECENT
EDITION OF THE ONE-FLY.

* * *

Above: THE GRAND TETONS
RISE ABRUPTLY WITHOUT BENE-
FIT OF FOOTHILLS, TOTALLY
DOMINATING THE LANDSCAPE
SURROUNDING THE SNAKE.

* * *

Opposite: SPORTING ARTIST
PETER CORBIN OF MILLBROOK,
NEW YORK, CASTS FROM THE
BOW OF A RIVER BOAT IN THE
DAYLONG HUNT FOR CUTTHROAT.

are free to get out of their craft and fish from shore and in waders. Each angler
is allowed to choose one fly to fish with and is out of the contest if he cannot
retrieve his fly or the fly is completely destroyed. Fish are caught on barbless
hooks, measured in inches, and then released unharmed back into the water.
The team that amasses the most points wins the contest.

"Some people may find the idea of competitive fly-fishing repugnant," says
Jackson Hole guide Jack Dennis, one of the tournament founders, "but this is
friendly competition and does not lose sight of what fly-fishing is all about,
the celebration of the outdoors," adding, "You're supposed to go fishing tense
and come back relaxed, anyway. If you come back a basket case, you've
missed the point."

The river, which flows south out of Yellowstone Park, opens for trout on
April 1, but heavy snow runoff from the Tetons keeps it high and roily until
late July or early August. Conditions are not always ideal for the contest. One
year it rained and snowed, forcing some of the anglers to leave the river, find
a laundromat, shed their wet clothing, and drink hot coffee and soup while
their clothes went through the drying cycle. Once reoutfitted, the hardy fishermen got back to the river and resumed their pursuit of the wily cutthroat.

In the history of the tournament, the only fly to win more than once has
been a streamer called the Double Bunny. The creation of Scott Sanchez, it is
crafted from two different colored rabbit pelts glued together, with eyes affixed
to the body. Intended to mimic a small wounded fish, the Double Bunny was
actually victorious three years in a row, from 1992 to 1994.

No cash prizes are awarded at the One-Fly, but the winners get trophies
and fishing gear. Trophies are named in memory of Bob Carmichael, a beloved
guide who operated the Tackle Shop, in Moose, Wyoming, one of the first fly
shops in the Rockies, from the late 1930s until his death in 1959, and Peter
Crosby, a popular Jackson Hole resident who tragically drowned at the age
of twenty while guiding for the inaugural One-Fly.

From a hand drawn map
By Adam

N
W ← → E
S

Coïque

Quimán   CAHUINAHUE   FLOR...

Rio Bueno
outlet to sea

LAGO
RANCO

CALCURRUPE

L. maihue

FURALELFU
Nilahue

Iliahue

RIÑINAHUE

Haig-Brown lists the following rivers in Fisherman's winter:

Rivers flowing into L. Ranco:
1. CALCURRUPE
2. Nilahue
3. Riñinahue
4. Cahuenahue (sic)
5. Quimán

Rivers flowing into L. Maihue:
1. Hueinahue
2. Carran
3. Rio Blanco
4. Quiniloilfu

Air temp fell into the 20s.

STREAM NOTES

THE EDUCATION OF AN ANGLER

JUST FOR FUN, Jim Brown was fishing what he calls his neighborhood river under the Main Street bridge in downtown Stamford, Connecticut, where he lives and works, as a cataloguer for Stamford's Ferguson Library. Passersby stared down at him incredulously as he threw out a small yellow panfish popper with his 9-foot four-weight fly rod, while cars and trucks roared past overhead.

In spite of being surrounded by tall buildings and busy roadways, Mill River is a charming little stream that flows about 10 miles from a reservoir north of the city through the urban heart of Stamford down to a harbor on Long Island Sound. Jim and fellow local conservationists had been working to get the city to recognize the importance of the river to a greenbelt proposal for the central city. Specifically, they wanted to see a fish ladder installed at the Main Street dam to help reestablish spring runs of native alewives and blueback herring. The same had been done with great success on the Mianus River in neighboring Greenwich. "The cost would be modest for the environmental gain that could be made," says Brown, who would like to see advocacy begin for the mill rivers found in almost every town in America. "If just a few people took an interest in every neighborhood river, it could make a huge difference."

On this day, Jim came home not with a fish (he releases virtually all the fish he catches) but with a black-and-white kitten he'd found abandoned and starving in a culvert at the river's edge. He and his wife, Pat, a high school English teacher and "cat person to the core," according to Jim, decided to name the cat Milton, after the river where he was found.

If nothing else, the cat story illustrates the hyperattentive, proactive stance Jim Brown takes whenever he gets near a river or stream. Ever since he caught his first trout in seventh grade, Brown has been scrupulously observing the fishing universe around him, both near at home and far away, in places like Chile,

Opposite: ALMOST TWENTY-FIVE YEARS AFTER HE WROTE IN HIS FIRST FISHING JOURNAL, CONNECTICUT LIBRARIAN JIM BROWN MADE EXTENSIVE NATURAL HISTORY NOTES ON HIS FIRST FLY-FISHING TRIP TO CHILE, WHERE HE FISHED THE CUMILAHUE AND CALCURRUPE RIVERS AND NOTED THAT EVEN IN THESE REMOTE AREAS THERE ARE CONSERVATION ISSUES.

* * *

Below: BROWN TAKES AS MUCH INTEREST IN HIS NEIGHBORHOOD STREAM, THE MILL RIVER OF DOWNTOWN STAMFORD,

CONNECTICUT, AS THE EXOTIC FISHING LOCALES HE HAS VISITED. JIM AND FELLOW CONSERVATIONISTS HAVE BEEN LOBBYING TO CREATE A FISH LADDER IN THIS URBAN STREAM TO HELP RE-ESTABLISH LOCAL FISH POPULATIONS THAT FORMERLY CAME UP THE RIVER FROM LONG ISLAND SOUND.

Top: A JOURNAL ENTRY FROM APRIL OF 1999 INCLUDES A DRAWING OF A CANADA GOOSE FEEDING ON MAYFLIES IN THE HOUSATONIC RIVER. BROWN USES THE WATER THERMOMETER TO TAKE THE TEMPERATURE OF EVERY STREAM HE FISHES.

* * *

Above: BROWN'S EARLIEST JOURNAL DATES FROM 1962, WHEN HE WAS THIRTEEN AND IN SEVENTH GRADE. IT RECORDS HIS FIRST TROUT, A 10-INCH BROOK TROUT CAUGHT IN THE STILL RIVER, WOODSTOCK VALLEY, CONNECTICUT.

* * *

Right: EGG FLIES FOR STEELHEAD AND SALMON WERE THE LURE OF CHOICE IN OCTOBER 1997, ACCORDING TO JIM BROWN'S JOURNAL OF A FISHING TRIP TO THE SALMON RIVER IN UPSTATE NEW YORK. "THE LEAVES MAY BE PAST THEIR PRIME BUT THEY'RE STILL A FINE SIGHT," HE WROTE AS AN ASIDE.

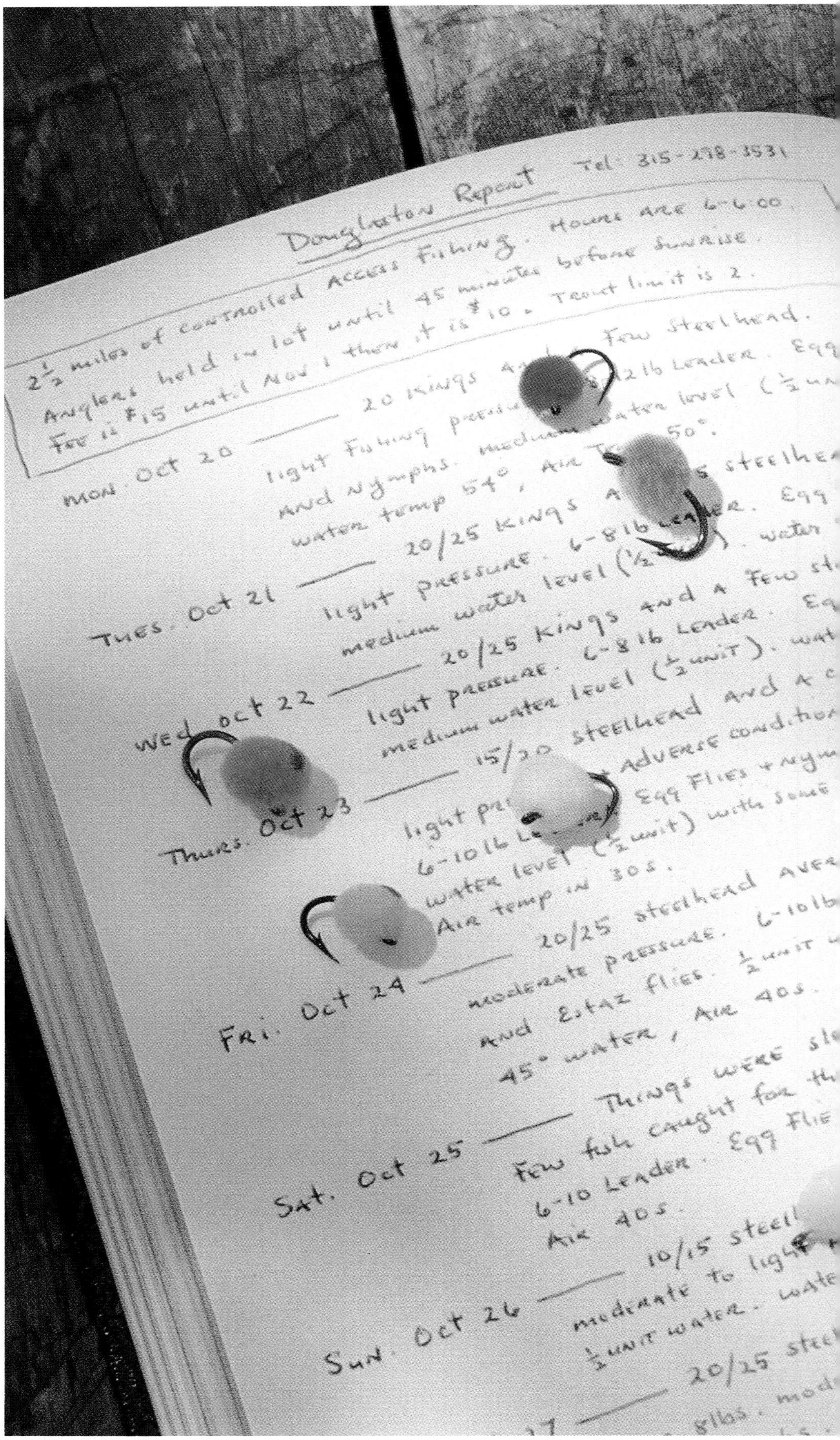

SAT. OCT. 18 ——
Beaverkill (Wagon Tracks) 55°, 4–5:30
Sunny + cool. The Leaves may be past their prime ...
three still a fine sight. Anglers in junction pool ...
Hendricksons, and Cairns Wagon Tracks is Free ...
give it a shot. The River is very low + clear.
Two modest size risers near midstream at ...
They ... and appear skittish, enough ...
Feed off our boat effort ... Do not see any ...
there are a few ... spinners Also ...
Caddis. There were ... of white ...
were getting on the water and three ...
what the Trout were taking. An invisible ...
... Fall day. Mac Francis

SUN. OCT 19 ——
28" (9½ lb.) steelhead ♀ — Yell...
Sunny, cool, a heavy mist on the ...
water all morning very heavy F...
Pressure: probably 200 cars. I ...
Areas on the River as follows:
15 Pineville Bridge, 30 Ellis C...
10 Upper Fly Area. Whitaker...
been boat screwed in 3 or 4 ...
A 22 lb steelhead landed ...
hours (7 days a week) acc...
½ gate, and the steelhe...
Faster runs. This Fish j...
and close to shore. ...
quickly turn it and ...
Measure + Release it. S...
post bright female w F...

http://www.whitakers.com

[left margin, partially visible]
... Air 40s
... head.
...ies.
54° Air 30s
...ple of Browns
(6" wet snow)
... medium
... off. water 52°,
... 4–8 lbs.
...adie. Egg Flies
...er. + some run off.
Today with relatively ...
effort applied.
½ unit water. 46° water,
... a few Kings.
Egg Flies + nymphs.
...ssure. Air 40s.
...emp 45°, Air 40s.
...d and a couple of Browns
...to light pressure. Egg Flies
...8/6 leader. ½ unit water.
Air temp. 40s.

Below: BEFORE HE BECAME A NATIONALLY RECOGNIZED AUTHORITY ON FLY REELS, BROWN LISTED IN HIS JOURNAL THREE REELS HE BOUGHT FROM TACKLE DEALER BOB LANG AFTER A LONG DAY OF FISHING IN CONNECTICUT. HIS RETURN TRIP FROM LANG'S, AFTER A LATE NIGHT OF TALKING TACKLE, SO EXHAUSTED HIM THAT HE LOCKED HIMSELF OUT OF HIS CAR THE NEXT DAY, FORCING A POSTPONEMENT IN HIS FISHING PLANS.

* * *

Bottom: BROWN'S FISHING JOURNALS FUNCTION LIKE A WELL-DESIGNED LANDING NET, CATCHING AND RELEASING INFORMATION ABOUT THE GAME OF FLY-FISHING WITHOUT LEAVING BRUISES ON THE TRUTH.

Above: BROWN HAS COLLECTED
A HOST OF COLORFUL AND
BIZARRE AMERICAN-MADE LURES
OF COMPOSITE MATERIALS, IN-
CLUDING WOOD, METAL, AND
PLASTIC, WITH VISAGES TO AMUSE
THE FISHERMAN, IF NOT THE FISH.

* * *

Below: BROWN TURNED TO
EXPERT CARVER STEPHEN SMITH
OF JAMESTOWN, NEW YORK, TO
CREATE THIS PORTRAIT OF
AN AMAZINGLY LARGE BROOK
TROUT HE CAUGHT IN
LABRADOR, CANADA.

England, and Quebec. For nearly thirty years he has kept a fishing journal of his angling adventures.

By the late 1970s, he had worked out his journal format, "not only record-ing the catch, but what I caught it on, where I was fishing, the water temper-ature, time put in, and some particulars of the day, including natural history elements such as the flies on the water," he relates. "My goal was to learn as much from each outing as I possibly could, to fully understand the fishing environment." Brown embellishes notes with his own illustrations, from com-parative portraits of the British and American kingfishers, to a pen-and-ink sketch of three antique fly reels he purchased from a friend.

When he is not making entries in his journal, Brown finds time to produce works of scholarship such as *A Treasury of Reels,* his exhaustive monograph on the fishing reel collection of the American Museum of Fly Fishing, pub-lished in 1990. He should know: Jim possesses one of the most important col-lections of antique fly reels in private hands. "I was able to get hold of many of the best reels before prices went through the ceiling," he confides. "Believe me, on a librarian's salary, I needed to have something like that going for me."

More recently, Brown turned his attention to collecting fly rod lures from the 1920s and 1930s, animated little fig-ures designed to grab a fish's attention, of which he now has more than 2,000 — "enough to give a good general overview of this amusing field."

8½ lbs. · MINIPI, WOODY'S INLET · #14 BLACK NOSE DACE · 1st SEPTEMBER, 1996 · JIM BROWN

On the image:
- Wright & McGill **Flying Moth** TRADE MARK "FLOATS" t and Bass MANUFACTURED BY W__T & McGILL DENVER COLO., U. S. A. World Famous Fishing Tackle PATTERN

- JOE MESSINGER'S BUCKTAIL FROG son I know of for leaving home." neth A. Reid M. ME

- WRIGHT & McGILL'S **HELGAMITE** TRADE MARK PATENT FOR BASS FOR TROUT Denver, Colorado, U. S. A. FLY ROD S__ No. HM-I 40¢ MADE IN U. S. A.

Left: A MENAGERIE OF FLY ROD
LURES FROM THE 1920S AND '30S
ILLUSTRATES THE ZANY APPEAL
OF THE PETITE ARTIFICIAL
CREATURES THAT, ONCE THEY
WERE DROPPED INTO THE WATER
AT THE END OF A FISHING LINE,
WERE EXPECTED TO EXCITE
THE INTEREST OF RAVENOUS
GAME FISH.

* * *

Below: JIM BROWN TIES A SMALL
BEAD-HEAD NYMPH, THINKING
THAT IF HE FISHES IT NEAR THE
BOTTOM OF MILL RIVER THIS
DAY, HE MIGHT GET A BITE.

RESOURCES

The Quest for Antique Tackle: A Dealer's View

BY KEN REBACK

UNTIL THE nineteenth century most fishing equipment used in America was imported from Great Britain, many examples of which can still be found in the basements and attics of homes along the eastern seaboard and the older cities of the interior. A growing demand for tackle and the burgeoning Industrial Revolution inspired the development of a truly American style of equipment designed to meet the demands of local fish and waters.

REELS

THE AMERICAN version of the fishing reel evolved in two distinct locations. The first was New York, where a heavy, rather primitive-looking device usually constructed of solid brass was produced primarily for saltwater species such as striped bass and bluefish. By the turn of the century the more creative manufacturers such as John Conroy, Julius vom Hofe, and Edward vom Hofe had refined the New York reel into a highly crafted, handmade creation of great beauty and function that is highly prized among today's collectors.

The second area of reel development was the state of Kentucky, where watchmakers and gunsmiths who had long been repairing imported reels put their metal-smithing talents to work and fashioned a reel for largemouth bass fishing. The result of their efforts was a machine of amazing precision and exquisite attention to detail.

Initially made of brass, the great majority of Kentucky reels were eventually constructed of German silver, a nickel-copper-zinc alloy which has become the standard for quality in antique fishing reel materials.

RODS

THE FISHING rods of America followed a similar pattern of development, evolving from the English-style solid wood rods of lancewood, greenheart, and hickory to the finely tapered split bamboo creations of Hiram Leonard of Highland Mills, New York, and his protégés Ed Payne, Hiram Hawes, and Fred Thomas. These newer rods were most often composed of six strips of bamboo tapered to a specific formula and glued together to form a much stronger and resilient tool than was possible with solid wood shafts. The fact that many contemporary anglers have forsaken fiberglass and graphite for older cane rods attests to the functional charm of these early examples of the rod maker's art.

LURES

THE FISHING lures of the New World also have their origins in the British Isles. The fly patterns used in America were initially those concocted for English brown trout and salmon, but eventually were modified to match the less sophisticated tastes of the brook trout and basses. The predecessor of the wooden plug was the Devon or Phantom minnow, a fish-shaped lure made of metal or leather used primarily for salmon fishing in the United States, but were also manufactured here to some extent. The first commercially produced wooden lure appeared in 1876 and inspired an avalanche of shapes, designs, and colors offered by a number of companies that were primarily located in a belt from upstate New York to Ohio and including Michigan. Not coincidentally this represents, to a great extent, the original range of largemouth and smallmouth bass.

FISHING TACKLE AS COLLECTIBLES

THE CITIES of New York, Philadelphia, and Boston became centers for the manufacture and retail of not only rods and reels but countless fishing-related items and paraphernalia such as gaffs, creels, flies, silk lines, bait boxes, and such. The great tackle houses of the late nineteenth century such as Abbey & Imbrie, Williams Mills & Son, John Krider, and Thomas J. Conroy were all well established in these locations.

Fishing tackle as a collectibles field began to grow in the 1970s primarily through the efforts of lure enthusiasts who founded the National Fishing Lures Collecting Club in 1976. This organization boasts more than 3,000 members representing every state and a number of foreign countries. Interest in other tackle items soon developed and many antique tackle shows popped up at locations across the country.

DETERMINING VALUE

IN SEEKING good buys in antique tackle, perhaps the most important thing to remember is that what was good in the past is good now. The highest-quality tackle was produced in the smallest quantities, and as a result is much harder to find. This means looking for quality in materials and craftsmanship in construction. It doesn't take long to develop an eye for these attributes. Cast German silver and brass as opposed to stamped nickel-plated metal both on reels and rod fittings often suggests higher quality. Reels handmade or machined to fine tolerances that operate with butter smoothness will generally be of more value than their hastily assembled counterparts. Split bamboo rods are usually more desirable than whole wood or metal rods.

Maker's name is an extremely important factor in determining tackle value. Early American fishing equipment was produced by a relatively small number of manufacturers. Much of this tackle was made for the trade—sold to a retailer without the maker's name on it, or even bearing the name of the retailer. Some manufacturers' products had distinguishing characteristics that enable experienced collectors to identify the source, but the maker's name on the item is always more desirable. The most important early reel makers to look for are John Conroy; the vom Hofes—Frederick, Julius, and Edward; Benjamin Meek; and Benjamin Milam. Later mass producers of reels were Pflueger, Hendryx, Montague, and Meisselbach, all collectible to some degree.

Rods without a maker's name are rarely of significant value. The name is generally engraved on the metal rod butt, applied as a decal or signed in ink at the base of the shaft. Some of the collectible early manu-

facturers are Thomas Chubb, H. L. Leonard, Hiram Hawes, and Fred Devine. Later rods such as those by C. F. Orvis, F. E. Thomas, Goodwin Granger, and E. W. Edwards can be more valuable and often remain in use for fishing today. The rods that command the highest prices are those handcrafted subsequent to World War II by highly respected individual makers whose output was very small and whose work is considered the epitome of the rod maker's art. This is a relatively small group which includes Pinky Gillum, Edward Everett Garrison, Paul Young, and Jim Payne. Their rods are both fishable and collectible, and in good condition sell for thousands.

When buying bamboo fly rods, one point to keep in mind is that rods longer than 8 feet are worth much less than the same make and model in a shorter length. There are two reasons for this. First, bamboo is much heavier than the modern graphite compositions, and in the longer rod lengths is much less enjoyable to cast. Second, nearly all antique rods were longer than 8 feet; therefore, the shorter rods are far more rare and much more sought after.

DETERMINING CONDITION

PERHAPS THE most important thing to be concerned with when buying old tackle is condition: The condition of an item can make a tremendous difference not only in its value but in its saleability as well. This is especially true of bamboo rods. Most rods were made in two or three sections plus an extra tip. With very few exceptions, all sections must be exactly the same length. A short section indicates a repaired break. One short tip can cut the value of a desirable rod in half. Two short tips can make it unsaleable. Reels should retain most if not all of their original finish, have no broken or replaced parts, and be in operating condition. Lures must have original paint with few chips.

Ultimately, the best criterion to use in making a buying decision is how much you like the article. If you don't have to spend the rent money to get it and can derive pleasure from owning or fishing with it, then it is certainly a wise purchase. A great deal of enjoyment can be gained by owning or fishing with tackle that is a hundred or more years old. It allows us to admire the craftsmanship of a time when work of high quality was the norm, to appreciate the evolution and development of modern tackle, and to share some of the experiences of our ancestors as they used this same tackle in pursuit of our favorite pastime.

Ken Reback, a marine biologist with the Massachusetts Division of Marine Fisheries, has been a dealer in antique tackle for more than a decade, and, when not looking for inventory, likes to fly-fish for striped bass and bird-hunt with his springer, Flash. This article appeared in the June 1997 *issue of* On the Water *and is reprinted with permission.*

Artists, Craftsmen, Collectors, Dealers & Shops

ALABAMA

H. Kelly Seibels
Seibels Sportsman's Den
P.O. Box 277
Owens Crossroads, AL 35763
(205) 725-2017
Fine art, furnishings, gear.

CONNECTICUT

Chet Reneson
Tanturmorantum Road
Lyme, CT 06371
(203) 434-2806
Sporting artist.

Christine Guille
Country & Cabin Antiques
162 Barnes Road
Stonington, CT 06378
(860) 535-0244
cwguille@aol.com
Dealer in quality antique rustic furniture and accessories.

The Compleat Angler
987 Post Road
Darien, CT 06820
(203) 655-9400
Fly-fishing gear, outdoor clothing, and angling books.

Jim Brown
97 Franklin Street
Stamford, CT 06902
(203) 324-5441
Collector, researcher, and appraiser of antique and classic fly-fishing tackle.

A. J. Fionda
Male Antique Decor
Roxbury, CT 06783
(860) 354-7088
Fine piscatoriana, rods, reels.

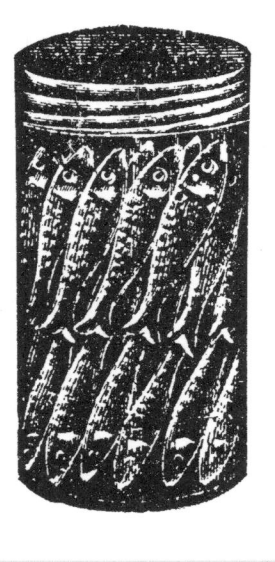

Frederick J. Balling
The Fishing Room
12 River Road
P.O. Box 87
West Cornwall, CT 06796
(860) 672-6809
Classic and used fly-fishing tackle, creels, lures, and gadgets; cabin furnishings, canoe items, folk art, sporting books, paintings, and prints. (Separate showroom at Housatonic River Outfitters in West Cornwall village.)

Scott Zuckerman
143 Whitcomb Hill
Cornwall Bridge, CT 06754
(860) 672-6032
Sporting artist.

COLORADO

Jim Pruitt and Shawn Collins
Lodge Camp 3
P.O. Box 21593
Boulder, CO 80308-4593
(303) 442-4094

Fishing and hunting antiques and rustic furnishings.

DELAWARE

John and Veronica Malchione
Malchione Antiques & Sporting Collectibles
110 Bancroft Road
Kennett Square, PA 19348
(610) 444-3509
Antique fly rods and reels, creels, fish decoys, lures, and folk art.

FLORIDA

Bob Berger
Bonefish Bob's
"Ye Old Tackle Shop"
81900 Overseas Highway
P.O. Box 56
Islamorada, FL 33036
(305) 664-9420
Old and new saltwater fishing tackle, flies, and books.

World Wide Sportsman & Zane Grey Lounge
81576 Overseas Highway
Islamorada, FL 33036
(305) 664-4615
Angling emporium, outfitter, travel agency, and atmospheric bar overlooking Florida Bay, all under one gigantic roof.

Sue and Gary Ellis
Redbone Gallery
200 Industrial Drive
P.O. Box 273
Islamorada, FL 33036
(305) 664-2002
Saltwater sporting art.

Capt. Jeffrey Cardenas
The Saltwater Angler
243 Front Street
Key West, FL 33040
(305) 296-0700
saltangler@aol.com
Sporting art, fly-fishing merchandise and fishing guide services, tropical outdoor clothing.

Capt. Dave and Pat Brown
The Tackle Box
1901 Overseas Highway
Marathon, FL 33050
captdave@thetacklebox.com
Bait, tackle, and free advice.

Biscayne Bay Fly Shop
8243 S. Dixie Highway
Miami, FL 33143
(305) 669-5851
BonefishFL@aol.com
Fly shop with sportswear and sporting art.

Everglades Angler Co.
810 Twelfth Avenue South
Naples, FL 34102
(941) 262-8228
mail@evergladesangler.com
Sporting art, fly rods, sportswear.

Bruce Miller
Kingfisher Art Gallery
Ocean Reef Club
82 Fishing Village Drive
North Key Largo, FL 33037
(305) 367-4410
Sporting art.

GEORGIA

Michael Paderweski
The Sportsman's Gallery, Ltd.
309 East Paces Ferry Road NE,
Suite 120
Atlanta, GA 30305
(404) 841-0133
Sporting art.

George and Mary Hedrick
George's Antiques
P.O. Box 82695

Atlanta, GA 30354
(770) 969-2061
Fish decoys, other fine antiques and collectibles.

Linda Davidson
American Antiques
296 Lakeshore Drive
Berkeley Lake, GA 30096
(770) 448-2773
Antique furnishings and angling accessories for lake, lodge, camp, and cottage. (By appointment.)

IDAHO

Robert Drummond
Drummond Gallery
The Coeur d'Alene, Suite A
Coeur d'Alene, ID 83814
(208) 772-9009
Western and sporting art.

McCoy's Tackle and Gift Shop
P.O. Box 210
Ace of Diamonds Street
Stanley, ID 83278
(208) 774-3377
Fly shop in oldest building in town, open May to mid-October.

ILLINOIS

Diane Lynwood Strong
Lynwood's of Livingston
County
14 Manor Drive
Pontiac, IL 61764
(815) 842-1687

Antique furniture and accessories including fly reels, bait boxes, and tackle catalogs.

INDIANA

Richard and Patricia Bouwkamp
Bouwkamp's Antiques
Brookston Antique Mall
Brookston, IN 47923
(765) 563-3505
Old Hickory and Adirondack furniture, rustic lamps, folk art, painted paddles, camp-scene pictures, and cabin rustica.

MAINE

Kittery Trading Post
Box 904, Route 1
Kittery, ME 03904
(207) 439-2700
info@ktp.com
Emporium for anglers, hunters, and campers.

John Bryan Fine Art
198 Milliken Road
North Yarmouth, ME 04097
(207) 829-6447
Artist/woodcarver who specializes in carved fireplace mantels, bas-reliefs, and sculpture with fishing motifs.

Bob Lang
31R Turtle Cove
Raymond, ME 04071
(207) 655-2493
Fishing tackle auctions.

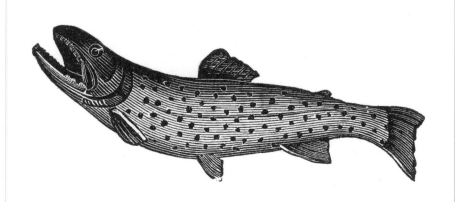

Bob Oestricher
  Moose America Antiques
  73 Main Street
  Rangeley, ME 04970
  (603) 431-4677
  Rustic and country antiques.

Tom Madden
  Mount 'n Sea Antiques
  32 Amesbury Street
  Rockland, ME 04841
  (207) 594-1761
  TBMadden@earthlink.net
  Rustic and fishing antiques.

Jon and Carla Magoun
  125 Ryerson Hill Road
  South Paris, ME 04281
  (207) 743-2040
  *Country furniture, folk art, and
  textiles.*

MARYLAND

C. D. Clarke
  P.O. Box 344
  Upper Fairmount, MD 21867
  (410) 651-9246
  *Sporting artist; oils, watercolors,
  and prints.*

MASSACHUSETTS

The Silver Panther Bait
  & Tackle Shop
  141 Buckland Road
  Ashfield, MA 01330
  (413) 628-0100
  *Fly-fishing and spinning tackle
  and supplies, angling antiques
  and collectibles.*

Scott McDowell
  The Copperworks of Martha's
  Vineyard
  RR 1, Box 314B
  Chilmark, MA 02535
  (508) 645-3131
  *Coppersmith (and charter fish-
  ing guide) specializing in hand-
  hammered models of striped
  bass, bluefish, salmon, and
  swordfish.*

Ross Bros.
  28 North Maple Street
  Florence, MA 01060
  (413) 586-3875
  *Antiques, wooden boats and
  canoes, architectural salvage and
  other unusual items.*

Snyder's Store
  945 South Main Street
  Great Barrington, MA 01230
  (413) 528-1441
  sasnyder@taconic.net
  *Rustic furniture, tramp art, and
  sporting trophies and mementos.*

Coffman's Country Antiques
  Jennifer House Commons
  Stockbridge Road/Route 7
  Great Barrington, MA 01230
  (413) 528-9282
  ccamjc@vgernet.net
  *Vintage angling gear, art, and
  collectibles*

J. Barry Thurston
  Barry Thurston's
  Harbor Square
  Nantucket, MA 02554
  (508) 228-9595
  Retail fishing equipment.

Ken Reback
  Sporting Antiquities
  11 Doten Road
  P.O. Box 1395
  Plymouth, MA 02360
  (508) 746-8584
  Vintage tackle, art, and books.

Richard E. Oinonen
  Oinonen Book Auctions
  P.O. Box 470
  Sunderland, MA 01375
  (413) 665-3253
  Sporting libraries.

Mara and Roy Superior
  8 Williams Street
  Williamsburg, MA 01096
  (413) 268-7904
  *Hand-painted, slab-built porce-
  lain vessels, platters, and relief
  pieces; wood furnishings, minia-
  tures, and constructions.*

MICHIGAN

Bob and Chris Rogers
  Rogers Antiques
  1135 Mason Road
  Dansville, MI 48819
  (517) 623-6566
  crogers@voyager.net
  *Rustic and sporting items
  including canoes, boat motors,
  primitives, log furniture, and
  cabin items.*

**WATCH
IT WIGGLE!**

Dick and Diane Elliott
   Elliott and Elliott Art &
   Antiques
   292 E. Third Street
   P.O. Box 751
   Harbor Springs, MI 49740
   (231) 526-2040
   *Early boat models, folk art,
   Native American art, textiles,
   carvings, pottery, furniture, and
   decorative items from the eigh-
   teenth century to the 1950s.
   (Open May through
   September.)*

Jerry Horan
   Logjam Art Studio
   23314 Seventeen Mile Road
   Leroy, MI 49655
   (231) 829-3727
   users.northlink.net/logjam/
   *Angling art and collectibles, rus-
   tic furniture and accessories.*

Bob Summers
   R. W. Summers Co.
   90 River Road East
   Traverse City, MI 49686
   (231) 946-7923
   RSummers@GTII.com
   *Builder of fine Tonkin cane fly
   rods; refinishes and repairs on
   all makes.*

MONTANA

Dan Bailey's Fly Shop
   P.O. Box 1019
   Livingston, MT 59047
   (800) 356-4052
   info@Dan-Bailey.com
   *Guided fly-fishing trips, fly-
   fishing gear and accessories, outdoor clothing, and gifts.*

NEW HAMPSHIRE

Bert Savage
   Larch Lodge
   Route 126
   Center Stafford, NH 03815
   (603) 269-7411

*Specializing in better forms of
rustic antiques, including furniture, sporting art, and accessories. (By appointment.)*

Phillip R. Crawford
86 High Street
Exeter, NH 03833
(603) 772-6669
*Collector of any items from
Abercrombie & Fitch and
Hardy Bros. Ltd.*

NEW YORK

Thomas Aquinas Daly
6365 East Arcade Road
Arcade, NY 14009
(716) 492-0846
Sporting artist.

Robert and Janet Sherwood
   Etcetera Antiques
   V-Corners at 987 Route 67
   Ballston Spa, NY 12020
   (518) 885-9393
   *Adirondack antiques, rustic and
   sporting, and nineteenth-
   century American folk art.*

Judith Bowman
The Uncaged Woman
   98 Pound Ridge Road
   Bedford, NY 10506

(914) 234-7543
*Rare and old books on angling,
hunting, and natural history.*

Henry Caldwell
   Black Bass Antiques
   Main Street
   Bolton Landing, NY
   (518) 644-2389
   *Adirondacks and Lake George
   antiques; specializing in antique
   fishing tackle.*

Pat and Butch Bramhall
   The Stonehouse Silversmiths
   RD 1, Box 312-9A
   Croghan, NY 13327
   (315) 346-1205
   *Hand-woven silver and gold
   creels, jewelry size through
   full size.*

Brian and Deborah Correll
   Correll Antiques
   Gloversville, NY 12078
   (518) 725-2049
   *Creels, baskets, and angling
   materials. (By appointment.)*

Stephen Smith
   47 Ellis Avenue
   Jamestown, NY 14701
   (716) 488-0139
   Fish-model carver.

George Jaque Antiques
Main Street, P.O. Box 545
Keene Valley, NY 12943
(518) 576-2214
Adirondack antiques and newly made rustic furniture.

Ralph Kylloe
Ralph Kylloe Gallery
P.O. Box 669
Lake George, NY 12845
(518) 696-4100
RKylloe@Capital.Net
New and antique rustic furniture and decorative cabin accessories.

Kenneth Seeber
Moose Brand Antiques
P.O. Box 327
Lowville, NY 13367
(315) 376-7133
Specializing in better forms of Adirondack antiques.

Skip and Lynn Gauger
15 Brayton Lane
Lake George, NY 12845
(518) 656-9248
Adirondack antiques and collectibles; early boats, motors, and marine art from lakes and rivers of the North Country.

Barney Bellinger
Sampson Bog Studio
171 Paradise Point
Mayfield, NY 12117
(518) 661-6563
Custom-designed tables, wall shelves, fly-fishing desks, cabinetry, and other rustic furnishings.

Peter Corbin
Shooter's Hill Press
RD 1, Box 128-B
Millbrook, NY 12545
(914) 677-5020
Sporting and landscape paintings, prints, and drawings.

Anglers & Writers
The Bespeckled Trout
420 Hudson Street
New York, NY 10014
(212) 675-0810
Restaurant and candy store at corner of St. Luke's Place with angling decor.

Urban Angler
118 East 25th Street
New York, NY 10010
(212) 979-7600
urbang@panix.com
Fly-fishing and some spinning gear, books, and art.

James Cummins Bookseller
699 Madison Avenue, 7th floor
New York, NY 10021
(212) 688-6441
cummins@panix.com
Sporting books and art.

Frank McNamara
Diamonds and Fly's, Ltd.
595 Fifth Avenue
New York, NY 10017
(212) 888-4677
flyshop@idt.net
Fine diamond jewelry pieces, fine fishing equipment, and custom-engraved boxes.

Nick Lyons
The Lyons Press
123 West 18th Street
New York, NY 10011
(212) 620-9580
Leading publisher of fly-fishing books, in addition to volumes on other topics in the sporting and natural history fields.

Hoagy Carmichael
Crosby Road
North Salem, NY 10560
(914) 277-8611
Vintage fly reels and bamboo fly rods.

Yvonne Miller
Miller Art & Frame
The Old 30 Main Building
3729 Main Street
Warrensburg, NY 12885
(518) 623-3966
Adirondack art, including local and rustic and birch framing, rustic furniture, and Adirondack camp accessories.

Mary K. Locke
Sherman & Locke
3729 Main Street
Warrensburgh, NY 12885
(518) 761-3156 or 494-5100
Adirondack and formal antiques and rustic collectibles, fine porcelain, silver, paintings, and prints.

NORTH CAROLINA

Jesse Brown's Outdoors
4732 Sharon Road, Suite 2M
Charlotte, NC 28210
(704) 556-0020
Outdoor speciality retailer, sporting art.

OHIO

Robert Burger
P.O. Box 765
Mt. Vernon, OH 43050
(740) 392-9101
Sporting collectibles and folk art paintings.

OKLAHOMA

Colonial Antiques
1329 East 15th
Tulsa, OK 74120
(918) 585-3865
Rustic furniture.

PENNSYLVANIA

Darryl and Karen Arawjo
   P.O. Box 477
   Sugar Mountain East
   Bushkill, PA 18324
   (570) 588-6957
   Custom-made fishing creels and baskets.

Ellen McCaleb
   308 Bridge Street
   Phoenixville, PA 19460
   (610) 917-1315
   ellen@fishcarvings.com
   Trophy fish carver and wildlife artist.

TEXAS

Collectors Covey
   15 Highland Park Village
   Dallas, TX 75205
   (214) 521-7880
   or (800) 521-2403
   Sporting art, wildlife art, and gifts for men.

David and Cathie Coleman
   West Bank Anglers
   5370 West Lover's Lane
   Suite 320
   Dallas, TX 75205
   (214) 350-4665
   Sporting art, fly-fishing outfitter.

Anteks
   2545 Kirby at Westheimer
   Houston, TX 77019
   (713) 526-4800
   Furniture, sporting and lodge accessories and art. (Other store locations: Dallas, San Antonio, Atlanta, Kansas City, and Los Angeles.)

Kathy Crow
   Crow & Co.
   2311 Westheimer
   Houston, TX 77098
   (713) 524-6055
   Accoutrements for the English country gentleman.

Nancy Bryant
   1022 Kern Street
   Houston, TX 77009
   (713) 864-3913
   nancy.bryant@bbs.hal-pc.org
   Platters, plates, and tiles painted with images of fish.

Sportsman's Edge
   Town & Country Mall
   800 W. Sam Houston Parkway
   Suite 221
   Houston, TX 77024
   (888) 463-9441
   Sporting art mainly geared to Texas

VERMONT

Bob Hoffman
   Moose River Lake
   and Lodge Store
   370 Railroad Street
   St. Johnsbury, VT 05819
   (802) 748-2423
   Fashions and furnishings for the home, lodge, camp, and cabin.

Robert Hutchinson
   Halcyon Meadow Antiques
   P.O. Box 41
   Bridgewater, VT 05034
   (802) 457-2181
   Old fishing tackle, camp and country antiques.

Orvis
   Route 7-A
   Manchester, VT 05254
   (800) 548-9548
   Flagship retail store for premier outfitter.

Andy Yager
   Vermont Trout Nets
   P.O. Box 1442
   Waitsfield, VT 05673
   (802) 496-5161
   akyager@aol.com
   Handcrafted catch and release nets with unique curved handle design allowing hands-free handling of the fish.

VIRGINIA

Murray's Fly Shop
   P.O. Box 156
   Edinburg, VA 22824
   (540) 984-4212
   murrays@shentel.net
   Local pharmacy doubles as outstanding tackle shop.

WYOMING

Jack Dennis Outdoor Shop
   50 East Broadway
   Jackson, WY 83001
   (307) 733-3270
   Fly shop, guide service, longtime sponsor of the One-Fly Contest.

Museums & Libraries

IGFA Fishing Hall of Fame and Museum
300 Gulf Stream Way
Dania Beach, FL 33004
(954) 922-4212
The International Game Fish Association's 50-acre Sportsman's Park includes a 60,000-square-foot interactive fishing museum, the fishing hall of fame, living wetlands exhibit, seven educational and historical galleries, a marina, an extensive research library, and the IGFA's administrative headquarters. Open daily.

Widener Library at Harvard University
Harvard Yard
Cambridge, MA 02138
(617) 495-2411
Daniel B. Fearing, 1915, Angling Collection: More than 11,500 volumes on angling, fishing, fisheries, and fish culture in 20 different languages, including more than 160 editions of the 170 editions of The Compleat Angler *published up to 1915; rare and early editions of some of the English poets; hundreds of books of travel; a long series of angling novels; more than 100 scrapbooks, each devoted to a single kind of fish; many cookbooks on fish; whaling treatises and log books; plus several thousand illustrations on the subjects of angling and fishes, including a series of 264 colored drawings of Chinese fish done on rice paper by a local artist.
John Bartlett, 1871, Angling Collection: Donated by the author of* Familiar Quota-*tions; more than 1,000 volumes on angling, many of them handsomely bound and ornamented in gold, and 269 pamphlets.*

Shrine of the Pines
Highway M-37
P.O. Box 548
Baldwin, MI 39304
(231) 745-7892
The rustic furnishings of master craftsman Raymond W. Overholzer on exhibit in a north woods log hunting lodge on the banks of the Pere Marquette River. Open May 15 to October 15.

International Fly Fishing Center
215 E. Lewis Street
Livingston, MT 59047
(406) 222-9369
Angling art, books, tackle, artifacts, aquariums, ecology displays, and gift shop.

Department of Rare Books and Special Collections
Princeton University Library
One Washington Road
Princeton, NJ 08544-2098
(609) 258-3184
Kenneth H. Rockey, 1916, Angling Collection: About 4,300 volumes, of which 350 are considered rare, with emphasis on American and English experience of angling in fresh and salt water; includes about 150 different editions of Izaak Walton's Compleat Angler.
*Otto von Kienbusch, 1906, Angling Collection: About 3,500 volumes, including the earliest angling book in Eng-*lish: *Dame Juliana Berners's A* Treatysse on Fysshynge Wyth an Angle, *printed by Wynkyn de Worde, assistant to England's first printer, William Caxton, in 1496; and the unique copy of the second angling book printed in English: (Anonymous)* The Arte of Angling, *London: Henry Middleton, 1577.*

The Adirondack Museum
Route 30
Blue Mountain Lake, NY 12812
(518) 352-7311
Exhibits on the life, work, and sporting pastimes in the Adirondack region of upstate New York, with over 450 paintings by A. F. Tait, Thomas Cole, Frederic Remington, and others. Library contains some 7,000 volumes and approximately 60,000 historic photographs.

Catskill Fly Fishing Center and Museum
P. O. Box 1295
Livingston Manor, NY 12758
(914) 439-4810
Flies, rods, reels, fly-tying desks, and many other artifacts of the Catskill Mountains' historic trout waters.

John L. Wehle Gallery of Sporting Art
Genesee Country Village & Museum
P.O. Box 310
Mumford, NY 14511
(716) 538-6822
gsvm@frontiernet.net
One of largest collections of sporting art in the country, with

more than 600 paintings, prints, and bronzes spanning four centuries.

International Hunting and Fishing Museum
P.O. Box 1028
Williamstown, NC 27892-1028
(252) 809-1795
themanagement@ihfm.org
Planned development calls for 500,000-square-foot museum and various outdoor facilities, including ponds stocked with bass, trout, and catfish, geared to instruction of young and novice anglers.

American Museum of Fly Fishing
Seminary Avenue and Route 7A
P.O. Box 42
Manchester Village, VT 05254
(802) 362-3300
Angling treasures on exhibit include antique rods and reels, thousands of noteworthy flies, art, prints, and ephemera.

National Fresh Water Fishing Hall of Fame and Museum
Box 33, Hall of Fame Drive
Hayward, WI 54843
(715) 634-4440
Collection includes some 5,000 lures, 400 fish mounts, and 300 classic outboard motors.

Angling On-Line

John A. Merry's 200 *Best Fly-fishing Web Sites* is a guide to fly-fishing sites on the Internet, including magazines and on-line publications, fishing suppliers, reports on weather and fishing conditions, and fly-fishing instruction, $15.95, published by: Specialized Marketing Agency, P.O. Box 218, Cameron Park, CA 95682.

American Fisheries Society
www.fisheries.org
Founded in 1870, AFS is the oldest and largest professional society representing fisheries scientists.

Atlantic Salmon Federation
www.asf.ca
Education and conservation group devoted to solving the plight of the diminishing Atlantic salmon.

Federation of Fly Fishers
www.fedflyfishers.org
FFF pursues conservation, habitat restoration, and education worldwide.

Theodore Gordon Flyfishers
www.users.interport.net/~trout
Conservation and fly-fishing group.

Trout Unlimited
www.tu.org/trout
Dedicated to conserving, protecting, and restoring North America's cold-water fisheries and their watersheds.

United States Fish and Wildlife Service
www.fws.gov
Information on American fisheries from government agency.

Fly-Fishing Women
w3.fly-fishing-women.com/flyfish
Includes club news from more than 30 women's fly-fishing clubs in the U.S.

Some regional sites:
Alaska Fly Fishers
www.akaflyfishers.org

California Trout
www.caltrout.org

StreamNet On-Line
www.streamnet.org
Pacific Northwest fishing.

Angling Destinations

John Ross and Katie Anders's *North America's Greatest Fishing Lodges* is a Sports Afield guide to more than 250 lodges, inns, camps, and resorts in the United States, Canada, and the Caribbean, $18.95, published 1997 by: Willow Creek Press, P.O. Box 147, Minocqua, WI 54548.

Robert Gartner's *The National Parks Fishing Guide* has information on fishing in 125 national parks throughout the United States and its territories, $14.95, published 1990 by: The Globe Pequot Press, Chester, CT 06412.

Lee and Mary Ann Graul
Fishing Creek Angler
314 St. Gabriels Road
Benton, PA 17814
(570) 925-2709
Fly shop.

Barry and Cathy Beck
Raven Creek Photography
309 Upper Raven Creek Road
Benton, PA 17814
(570) 925-2392
Fly-fishing trips, fishing school, and commercial photography.

Ron Hickman
Hickman Expeditions
P.O. Box 671004
Marietta, GA 30066-0134
(770) 977-5627 or 977-2072
Trips for anglers.

Mike Miller
West Bank Anglers Michigan
6612 Telegraph Road
Bloomfield Hills, MI 48301
(248) 538-FISH (3474)
Trips for anglers.

World Wide Sportsman
81352 Overseas Highway
Islamorada, FL 33036
(305) 664-9271
Saltwater fishing outfitter.

Seascape Ocean Resort
76th Street
Marathon, FL 33050
(305) 743-6455
seascapem@aol.com
Secluded small resort on a former private estate overlooking the bonefish flats of the Middle Keys.

Capt. Albert Ponzoa
203 Camino Real
Marathon, FL 33050
(305) 743-4074
Guide for Florida game fish, spin or fly.

Cabbage Key
P.O. Box 200
Pineland, FL 33945
(941) 283-2278
Small island resort in Pine Island Sound off the Gulf Coast near Fort Myers, with Old Florida accommodations and ambience and year-round saltwater fishing action.

Twin Farms
Barnard, VT 05031
(802) 234-9999
Luxury country hotel. The Perch, with its angling theme, is one of seven uniquely styled cottages on the property, along with six other premier accommodations and a well-stocked trout pond. Shaun and Beverley Matthews, managing directors.

Johnsons' Pere Marquette Lodge
Route 1, Box 1290
Baldwin, MI 49304
(231) 745-8010
pmlodge@carrinter.com
Full-service lodge, outfitter, and guide service on the Pere Marquette River.

Gates Au Sable Lodge
471 Stephan Bridge Road
Grayling, MI 49738
(517) 348-8462
gator@gateslodge.com
Motel-style inn on the Au Sable River, with fly shop, conference room, and restaurant.

The Gray Drake
7616 S. Hazelwood
Newaygo, MI 49337
(231) 652-2868
Fly-fishing, guide service, and lodging on the Muskegon River.

Brooks Lake Lodge
458 Brooks Lake Road
Dubois, WY 82513
(307) 455-2121
or (800) 678-6543
Historic lodge astride the Continental Divide, with fly-fishing and hunting base camps.

Flying A Ranch
Route 1, Box 7
Pinedale, WY 82941
(307) 367-2385
Historic ranch built in 1929 with lodge, six hand-crafted log cabins, and two large stream-fed ponds sporting rainbow and brook trout.

Sources for Collectors

**Adirondack Museum
Antiques Show**
Oliver and Gannon Associates
P.O. Box 651
Altamont, NY 12009-0651
(518) 861-5062
shows@albany.net

**American Fish Decoy
Association**
c/o John E. Shoffner, Director
624 Merritt
Fife Lake, MI 49633
(616) 879-3912
Publishes quarterly newsletter,
The American Fish Decoy
Forum, *and holds two shows a
year. Annual membership: $25.*

**Florida Antique Tackle
Collectors, Inc.**
P.O. Box 420703
Kissimmee, FL 34742-0703
*Nonprofit group organized to
enhance and promote the collection, preservation, and knowledge of old or antique angling
memorabilia and the history of
tackle produced in Florida; the
group conducts four shows a year
and publishes a quarterly newsletter. Annual membership: $20.*

**Great Lakes Fish Decoy
Collectors & Carvers
Association**
c/o Frank Baron, Secretary/
Treasurer
35284 West Chicago
Livonia, MI 48150
(734) 427-7768
*Dedicated to the preservation,
promotion of, and education
about the ice-fishing decoy as
functional and collectible American folk art. Publishes newsletter
and sponsors annual Fish Decoy
Carving World Championship.
Annual membership: $25.*

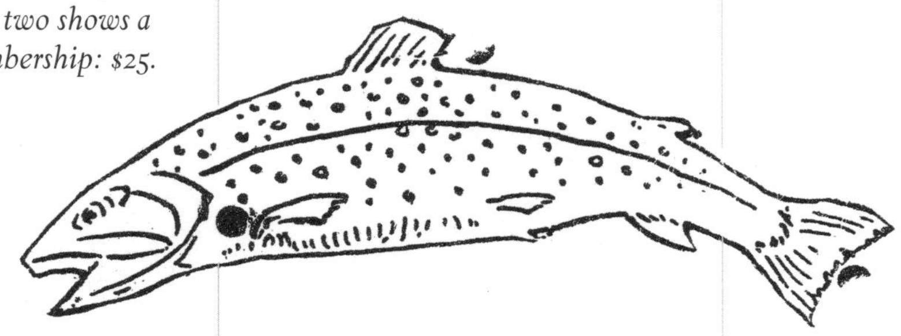

Books for Collectors

Carl F. Luckey's *Old Fishing Lures
& Tackle* is the fifth edition of the
identification and value guide to
fishing reels, old rods, and early
fishing lures; 752 pages, 1999,
$29.95 (paperback); available
from: Krause Publications, 700
E. State Street, Iola, WI 54990-
0001; (715) 445-2214.

Donna Tonelli's *Top of the Line
Fishing Collectibles* is an
overview of collectible fishing
paraphernalia, including fishing
lures, fish decoys, winter ice-
fishing equipment, fishing reels,
and related folk art, with a value
guide; 160 pages, 1997, $44,
available from: Schiffer Publishing, Ltd., 4880 Lower Valley
Road, Atglen, PA 19310; (610)
593-1777; schifferbk@aol.com.

A. J. Campbell's *Classic & Antique
Fly-fishing Tackle* is a guide for
collectors and anglers; 360
pages, 1997, $50; available from:
The Lyons Press, 123 W. 18th
Street, New York, NY 10011,
(212) 620-9580.

INDEX